THE ANXIETY BOOK
FOR TRANS PEOPLE

by the same author

Trans Love
An Anthology of Transgender and Non-Binary Voices
Edited by Freiya Benson
ISBN 978 1 78592 432 3
eISBN 978 1 78450 804 3

of related interest

Trans Power
Own Your Gender
Juno Roche
ISBN 978 1 78775 019 7
eISBN 978 1 78775 020 3

The Trans Self-Care Workbook
A Coloring Book and Journal for Trans and Non-Binary People
Theo Lorenz
ISBN 978 1 78775 343 3
eISBN 978 1 78775 344 0

Yes, You Are Trans Enough
My Transition from Self-Loathing to Self-Love
Mia Violet
ISBN 978 1 78592 315 9
eISBN 978 1 78450 628 5

The
Anxiety Book for Trans People

How to Conquer Your Dysphoria, Worry Less and Find Joy

Freiya Benson

Jessica Kingsley Publishers
London and Philadelphia

First published in Great Britain in 2021 by Jessica Kingsley Publishers
An Hachette Company

1

Disclaimer: The information contained in this book is not intended
to replace the services of trained medical professionals or to be a
substitute for medical advice. You are advised to consult a doctor on
any matters relating to your health, and in particular on any matters
that may require diagnosis or medical attention.

A CIP catalogue record for this title is available from the British Library
and the Library of Congress

ISBN 978 1 78775 223 8
eISBN 978 1 78775 224 5

Printed and bound in Great Britain by TJ Books Limited

Jessica Kingsley Publishers' policy is to use papers that are natural,
renewable and recyclable products and made from wood grown
in sustainable forests. The logging and manufacturing processes
are expected to conform to the environmental regulations
of the country of origin.

Jessica Kingsley Publishers
Carmelite House
50 Victoria Embankment
London EC4Y 0DZ

www.jkp.com

MIX
Paper from
responsible sources
FSC® C013056

Contents

Disclaimer 7

Introduction 9

Anxiety notes: Describe anxiety in a sentence 24

1. Things People Have Told Me about Anxiety:
   A Myth-Busting Guide 25

   On Anxiety – Sabah 37

2. Can I Fix My Anxiety? 41

   On Anxiety – Eris 54

3. Anxiety and Other Emotions 57

   Anxiety notes: What makes you anxious? 72

4. Coming Out 75

   On Anxiety – Rory 83

5. Dysphoria, Gender, Identity and Anxiety 87

   On Anxiety – Roch 102

6. Social Anxiety   105

    Anxiety notes: What do you do to make anxiety better?   115

7. Getting What You Need from Life   117

    On Anxiety – Maeve   128

8. Medical Services and How to Cope with Them   133

    On Anxiety – Meg-John (MJ)   141

9. Finding Joy   145

    On Anxiety – Effie   153

10. Practical Things We Can Do   157

11. Endings, Beginnings and How to Make It Better   193

    The Anxiety Toolkit   199

    Further Reading and Resources   201

    Bread for Anxious People   205

    Contributor Biographies   209

    Index   213

Disclaimer

For the purposes of this book, I'm going to be using the words 'trans' and 'transgender' quite a bit. I'm using them as umbrella terms, to try and cover the wide range of non-cis identities out there. I identify as a trans woman, so some of the things I write about are going to be coming from that perspective, but I've tried to include and acknowledge other identities where I can.

It's also worth mentioning that the ideas and thoughts in this book are just that: ideas and thoughts. I'm not saying that what I do is also what you should do to tackle your anxiety, but rather I'm offering some ways that might work for you or at least give you a starting point on your own journey with anxiety.

I hope this book helps in some way, so let's begin!

Introduction

This is a book about anxiety.

It's also a book about how that affects us as transgender, or trans, people. It's a big and complex subject, so we'll try and unpick it a bit, offer some ways forward, and hopefully all learn about what exactly is going on when anxiety gets its sneaky claws into us.

Anxiety isn't an easy thing – both in terms of writing about it and thinking about it – in part because it is such a huge subject but also because it affects us all in very different ways. One person might find crowds overwhelming, whilst another might have major anxiety around relationships or work. Some of us might have anxiety that we can mostly keep under control, whilst others will be completely disabled by theirs.

It's good to recognize this, because it also means there's no single solution or cure-all for anxiety. There are, however, some things that work better than others, and finding out what these things are is going to be a large part of what I'm going to cover here.

It's important to point out that this is going to be a book based around personal experiences. I'm not a doctor or a scientist or someone who's dedicated their entire life to studying anxiety, so if you're looking for something more science-based, then you probably won't find it here.

If, however, you're looking to find out more about real-life experiences from people who are maybe going through some similar types of stuff to you, then maybe, just maybe, this book might be for you!

As well as my own perspectives, this book will include other people's. There will be short sections, handily titled *Anxiety notes*, filled with quotes and thoughts from other trans and non-binary people, in response to particular questions about how they manage their anxiety.

Some of the stuff in this book might seem sort of basic, or obvious, but often the most effective ways of dealing with things are the simplest ways. There is great power in simplicity, and, actually, over-complicating things can often just lead to more anxiety!

Hopefully, you'll find some useful tips and ways of managing anxiety within these pages. Just so you know, all these methods have been tried and tested, either by myself or other trans people I know, because although it's important to talk about when and why, it's also really important to talk about what we can do to make things better.

What I'm all about

So, hi, I'm Freiya! I'm a writer and author, and I'm super-anxious a lot of the time.

I'm also trans, which is something I'm very proud of, but

it can also make my anxiety a bit of a mare sometimes. I say 'sometimes', but I really mean quite a lot of the time.

I can't remember the first time I felt anxious but I know anxiety like an old friend. It's been a presence in my life for as long as I can remember, both pre- and post-transition.

Sometimes I feel it less and sometimes it's so powerful and overbearing that I think I'm going to die. It's always present, though, like a siren from an ambulance, barely audible in the distance. 'You'd better be ready,' it wails, 'because I'm coming. You don't know when, or how, but someday soon something is going to happen and then BAM! I'm back, baby, your old friend anxiety.'

And the thing is, there are so many ways anxiety can happen. It's triggered by a multitude of events, scenarios and feelings. It sometimes (often) feels inescapable, acting as this consistent and harsh voice in your head, always ready to chip in and knock you down, screaming warnings about everything, and just basically tricking you into expecting the worst possible outcome for everything you do. Like I said before, it's a bit of a mare.

The when and who of anxiety

So, what is anxiety exactly?

Well, for starters, it's completely normal and it's been happening like forever. Anxiety isn't a new thing – it's just that the language around it has evolved.

Hippocrates (an ancient Greek physician) wrote about anxiety over 2000 years ago in the Hippocratic Corpus. In it, he writes about a man called Nicanor, who loved a good party. Unfortunately for Nicanor, whenever he went to one of these get-togethers, he started getting very bad anxiety every time the flute-girl started playing. As soon as he heard the sound of the flute, a terrible fear took over him. He said that he could hardly bear it, especially at night, and that these symptoms continued to persist over a long period of time. For Nicanor, this wasn't ideal as he really loved a good party, but his anxiety was kind of ruining things for him.

This was one of the earliest written examples of someone suffering from anxiety but it certainly wasn't the only one from ancient times. In Greek and Latin literature, the philosophers and scientists of the time would write about *angor*, or anxiety, as we now know it. They would write about the way *angor* affected people, often describing it as a constricting and narrowing disorder, which is actually pretty relatable. This is where the English word 'anxiety' comes from originally: the Latin word *angor* (roughly meaning mental anguish, distress or torment, or to constrict), along with the related word *angustus* (which roughly means narrow).[1] The idea of narrowness and anxiety also appears in Hebrew in the Bible, where Job (famous for being a prophet and being tested by God quite a lot) talks about the narrowness (*tsar*) of his spirit in relation to his anguish, which was brought about by all the testing of his faith (Job 7:10). Going forward in time a little, the word evolves into the Latin *anxietas*, and the German word *Angst*.

Back in Hippocrates' day, people also wrote about ways that you could free yourself from the effects of anxiety, often describing techniques we still use today, such as trying to live a carefree life, living in the moment and following the path of Stoicism.

Stoicism isn't something you'd necessarily think about in terms of helping with anxiety, but it's something that is surprisingly relevant to our ways of being in today's world. Stoicism says that how we behave affects our happiness and that the key to happiness is to behave in a virtuous way. Basically, try

---

1   See https://en.wiktionary.org/wiki/anxiety.

to be kind and nice, even when things get tough. The thinking behind this is that we don't always have control over the external events and occurrences that affect us, but what we do have is control over ourselves and how we respond to things. Stoicism is sometimes described as not being about complicated theories or debates but rather about finding ways to overcome destructive emotions, such as anxiety or depression, and doing what we realistically can to make things better.

Basically, as the ancient Greek philosopher and founder of Stoicism, Zeno of Citium, famously may or may not have once said, 'We can't do shit about a lot of stuff that happens, so just chill, go with the flow and be nice.'

Everyone experiences anxiety at some point, even if they try to tell you otherwise. Anxiety is everywhere. And it affects everyone. Seriously. Even those people that seem like they're super-together and are amazingly confident. I hear you, though. You want examples, right? Well, take a look at this list I've shamelessly compiled from 20 minutes of googling 'super-together amazingly confident celebrities who have anxiety':

- Oprah Winfrey, famous chat show host, who spoke about how her anxiety nearly led to her having a nervous break-down.

- Kim Kardashian West, reality star who has spoken about her anxiety and its relationship to trauma.

- Kristen Stewart, actor, most famously known for the *Twilight* films, who had panic attacks and stomach aches when she was younger.

- Missy Elliot, American singer-songwriter, rapper, producer and dancer, who had an extreme panic attack before her 2015 Superbowl performance.

- Kristen Bell, actor, known for *Veronica Mars* and, more recently, the amazing *The Good Place*, who has spoken about taking medication for anxiety and depression.

- David Beckham, sports superstar, who opened up about his obsessive compulsive disorder (OCD) and the anxiety it causes him.

- Laverne Cox, activist and actor, who spoke about the trauma she experiences as a transgender woman of colour, the pressures of her work, and how she uses self-care to help relieve anxiety.

- Lady Gaga, American singer-songwriter and actor, who has suffered from anxiety and depression for most of her life and set up the Born This Way Foundation to help people through their mental health issues.

- Michael Phelps, Olympic swimmer, who experienced struggles with anxiety, depression and suicidal thoughts.

- Ryan Reynolds, Canadian actor, famously known for starring in *Deadpool*, who spoke about how he used humour to try and cope with his anxiety.

- Prince Harry, famous member of the British Royal Family, who spoke about seeking counselling to help with the anxiety and grief he felt after the death of his mother, Diana, Princess of Wales.

- Leonardo DiCaprio, American actor, famous for loads of films, including *Titanic*, who has spoken about his OCD and anxiety.

- Hugh Grant, British actor, famous particularly for starring in various British romantic comedies, who experiences panic attacks.

And then there are all the people from history as well. We can't directly ask them if they had anxiety, but all the evidence points to the fact that they experienced it:

- Abraham Lincoln, famous American president, whose anxiety disorder we know about through the letters and journals he wrote.

- Emily Dickinson, beloved poet, who also limited most of her interactions with others to letters and became more and more reclusive as she got older. Experts have theorized that she suffered from anxiety, and likely agoraphobia.

- Vincent Van Gogh, who made some amazing art. In his letters he wrote about his fits of anxiety and attacks of melancholy.

- Charles Darwin, known for discovering evolution, was super-reclusive, and after his famous voyages he barely left his home. Recent research suggests that he had agoraphobia, and panic disorder.

- Georgia O'Keeffe, an American artist known for her beautiful paintings of flowers, amongst other things. She was admitted to hospital suffering from anxiety and depression, describing symptoms such as not eating, and struggling to sleep. Interestingly, a hospital stay didn't work for Georgia; instead, what really helped was travelling and getting away from the sources of anxiety that were affecting her.

Some people will use different words to describe anxiety or hide it behind bravado and bluster. Some will even outright deny it as even being a thing. They'll say it's just the younger generation being 'snowflakes', that anxiety is a modern affliction, and that back in their day everyone just got on with it. (We'll come back to this later on, along with some other classic myths and preconceptions about anxiety.)

They're wrong, obviously, and now you know the evidence that says otherwise. If anyone disagrees, tell them Hippocrates wants a word with them. We've known about anxiety for centuries – it's one of humankind's oldest companions. The triggers, the language and the thinking behind it may have changed and evolved, for sure, but it's always been there.

Anxiety, basically

So, anxiety is, simply put, your body's way of telling you that something is off, or not right. This can manifest in a lot of different ways, but basically, anxiety is a persistent feeling of worry, nervousness or fear.

Anxiety in many situations is very important. It's our body's early warning system kicking in, alerting us to danger or threat, and it's there to help us, even if sometimes it feels otherwise. Anxiety is important to our survival, and in the early days of human existence it would have alerted us to dangerous, bitey predators, allowing us to escape danger. This feeling gives us an adrenaline rush, making us more sensitive to what's happening around us, getting our muscles ready to respond and giving us a potentially much-needed burst of energy which allows us to escape or kick off against whatever is giving us trouble. The American physiologist Walter Bradford Cannon wrote about this in the early 1900s, coining the term 'fight or flight response'. Interestingly, this reaction (also known as the acute stress response, or hyperarousal) is something that happens to a whole range of different animals.

Nowadays, of course, there's less in the way of natural predators to give us stress, but there are still things that will trigger this response, be that work, health, family or our identity, for example. Unfortunately, in a lot of these modern situations the old fight or flight response isn't very helpful. Our bodies and minds, however, only know this primitive response to perceived threats, and so it still kicks in, creating anxiety.

For example, a while back I got asked to be on a panel for a magazine I was writing for at the time. They wanted me to talk about sex and relationships, something I knew quite a bit about, so I said yes, thinking that it would be fine. Now, a couple of months before the actual event everything *was* fine (well, fine in a 'It's a long way off, so that little seed of anxiety I'm already feeling probably will just go away' kind of fine).

Of course, though, the closer it got to the event, the more anxious I started to feel. I looked up the other people who were on the panel with me, which was a big mistake. They were all, according to my anxious brain, so much better and so much more qualified than me. My imposter syndrome kicked in big time, and I started panicking. In my head I was all like 'I'm literally nobody, just some random person that said something about being trans once that some people thought was insightful.' It was quite probably just a fluke on my part, so asking me to repeat that, on this panel, with actual legit people was, in my head, a huge mistake.

That seed of anxiety, the little tiny one I felt back when they asked me to do this, was starting to sprout...and it was having a growth spurt.

On the actual evening of the event, I just wanted to run away. I foolishly didn't allow myself enough time to write anything down because of my anxiety, so when I started speaking I was trying to do it off the top of my head. This in turn made me more anxious, and it showed.

Readers, it was not my finest hour.

I managed to do it, just about, but I left as soon as I could, because I needed to get away. I needed to take flight. In my mind, what I said (and actually the whole experience) was so awful that I've never felt able to speak on a panel again. It was such a strong and overpowering feeling that even though I actually managed to do the panel, even though I managed to do something that gave me major anxiety, it just wasn't enough. Even now, years later, my anxiety still kicks in and tells me that I should never do that again. 'You just about got by that time,' it says, 'but next time you might not be so lucky, so maybe just DON'T EVER DO THAT AGAIN.'

The problem a lot of us have is that sometimes it's very hard to tell if the threat is real, or if the reaction you're having is proportional to the perceived threat. Take the example I just wrote about. I felt anxious but I still managed to do it. Logically, that suggests that I should be able to do that sort of thing again, but my anxiety reaction is all about the 'No, you need to never do that again.' My anxiety reaction is basically disproportional and not based on any of the reality of what actually happened. It's only now, looking back, that I can see this. At the time (and for a long while afterwards if I'm being truthful), when my heart was racing and my thoughts were running away in unhelpful and irrational directions, it was very hard – almost impossible, in fact – to also assess what was really going on. Anxiety is very consuming and very noisy. It doesn't leave space for much else other than worry and fear, and it doesn't take much before you find yourself really stuck, going round and round in ever-decreasing circles.

Over time, and especially if this happens regularly, it can start to become your body's way of managing anxiety, and then it becomes a problem, as you react badly no matter what the anxiety is warning you about, be it a spider, talking in front of some people or actual imminent death.

Anxiety and anxiety disorders

In this book we're going to be talking about anxiety a lot – it's what the book is about, after all – so we should probably also talk about the difference between anxiety and anxiety disorders.

Anxiety is something we all experience, but if that anxiety continues, feels out of proportion to the threat or situation occurring, and also starts to impact and affect your day-to-day life, it could be an anxiety disorder.

Anxiety disorders can be further broken down into a variety of types, the most common being:

- generalized anxiety disorder, or GAD for short

- social anxiety (a long-lasting, often overwhelming fear of social situations)

- phobia-based anxiety (e.g. nyctophobia, the fear of the dark)

- panic disorder (where you regularly have sudden panic or fear attacks)

- post-traumatic stress disorder, or PTSD for short (a type of anxiety caused by extremely stressful or frightening events).

There are other types as well, but these are the ones that are most likely to come up if you go to the doctor and they diagnose an anxiety disorder.

When you experience mild anxiety, it can be unsettling and weird, but severe anxiety can affect everything.

If you're doing an exam, and it's getting quite stressful, then that's anxiety. If these feelings persist or feel uncontrollable, leading to a panic attack or stopping you from being able to attend other future exams, then maybe your anxiety has developed into an anxiety disorder.

Anxiety disorders can hugely affect your life, making it difficult to do things like hold down a job, have a relationship, look after yourself and ultimately just enjoy life.

(Obviously, like I said before, I'm no doctor, so if you feel like all this talk about anxiety disorders is sounding a bit too close to home, then you should speak to a GP, if you can, to get an official diagnosis.)

Anxiety and trans people

So, anxiety. It's out there and it's messing things up for us all. For some of us, though, it's *really* messing things up.

As a trans person, my anxiety has some extra facets to it that are a direct consequence of me being trans. A lot of this has its roots in anxiety that other people experience; it's just that being trans often adds another layer to it, rather like a really weird cake that you would never want to eat.

Let's take a look at a non-cake-based example, using one of the most common triggers for anxiety.

You've been invited to a party! If you don't experience anxiety you're probably all like BRING IT ON, but if you get social anxiety, for instance, this is going to cause some problems.

So, a while back, the house share I lived in decided that they'd like to throw a house party. Now, there's a part of me that wishes that I could just rock up and be the life and soul – like witty conversation, dancing on tables, centre-stage getting on the karaoke like a queen type of stuff.

However, there's a bigger part of me that is just OH NO, NOT THIS AGAIN because of social anxiety.

The basic anxiety level is that being in busy crowded places spins me out, and I get panicky and anxious. The trans anxiety level is that I know my being trans has the potential to make this unsafe.

There are going to be people I know at this party, and there are going to be people I don't as well. The people I know I can just about deal with, but the others are a new and unpredictable factor. I don't know much, if anything, about them, and I don't know how they feel about trans people. I don't know how they feel about me. That probably sounds a little self-absorbed, right? Like maybe they just don't care about me and it'll all be fine. Maybe I don't need to worry about this, maybe I'm being ridiculous. Except, in today's world a lot of what people know about trans people is very polarized. From my experience, people often have quite strong, and often ill-informed, opinions about trans people, which gives me a lot of anxiety. Other people's potential reactions to me, my identity and my existence give me anxiety.

I don't know if that person over there hates trans people or not. I don't know if this guy flirting with me even realizes I am trans, and I don't know what he's going to do when he does realize.

I don't know if the people I do know are going to accidentally out me, with a casual 'Hey, this is Freiya. She's trans,' or if someone is going to come up to me and just plain old ask outright, 'Are you trans?'

I dread the moments when someone spots you as trans and

then decides to have a conversation about trans people within earshot.

I hate the times where you notice a group of people looking at you, where it's obvious they're talking about you, and you catch their eyes and they all look away awkwardly.

I hate being the only trans person here. That makes me anxious. Being the only one in a crowd always makes me anxious.

I hate finally plucking up the courage to talk to someone, only for them to do a double-take at my voice and, worse, comment on it.

Being trans makes base-level anxiety so much worse, because being trans opens up so many new possibilities for anxiety to be amplified, exaggerated and expanded. It gets tricky very quickly because so much of life involves interacting with other people, but so much of my anxiety as a trans person is about how other people react to my trans identity when we do interact.

I know that this makes it all sound a bit hopeless and depressing. Anxiety and being trans have felt deeply entwined for so many of us right from the start, which can then make overcoming anxiety very difficult. It's no surprise that in a recent Stonewall survey (the LGBT in Britain Health Report 2018)[2] 71 per cent of trans people, and 79 per cent of non-binary people said they experienced anxiety.

It's very clearly something that a lot of us know and live with, and that a lot of us really struggle to manage.

Unfortunately, the thing about anxiety is that it can often be all-consuming. It doesn't leave much space for anything else, like developing creativity or seeing friends or having fun times. It doesn't leave space to do something about it. This is

---

2   Stonewall (2018) 'LGBT in Britain: Health.' Available at www.stonewall.org.uk/resources/lgbt-britain-health-2018.

why isolation and anxiety often go hand in hand. Anxiety is all about the NO, and that's not always helpful.

It gets so messed up sometimes that it becomes hard to see a way through and we just get stuck in a loop, feeling anxious about everything, including trying to do something about it.

We can get out of it though. We just need to stop for a moment and ask ourselves one simple question: '*Do I want to feel like this?*'

It's a very simple question, but it's also one of the most important questions we can ask ourselves, because if it turns out that actually, no, you don't want to feel like this, then the next most important question you need to ask yourself is this: '*What can I do to change that?*'

And that, my friends, is what this book is all about.

Anxiety notes: Describe anxiety in a sentence

Anxiety is a vibrating, gut-wrenching and catatonic (or twitchy) state of utter despair.

Anxiety makes everything more difficult to do because my tummy and heart say I should be nervous about everything.

My brain goes on high alert and I become fixated on the source of anxiety and then struggle to stop.

Anxiety is a sick feeling in my tummy, making me need to go to the loo over and over again.

Anxiety is a reminder that I'm not completely healed.

Anxiety is all my bad experiences and feelings rising up at once, overwhelming any possibility of being in the present moment or acting with thought for the future.

Anxiety is an uncomfortable feeling on a spectrum from worry to panic: frightened and fragile, tense and fluttery inside, something's not right.

It's that feeling of tension, like a knot in your stomach that tries to push itself up inside you, squeezing your heart, tightening your throat, making you panic.

Anxiety for me is being scared of everything.

Anxiety is almost too much to bear in the moment, but such a relief when it leaves, even if it's just for a time.

Anxiety is walking down the street, hearing people laughing, and worrying that they're laughing at me.

CHAPTER 1

Things People Have Told Me about Anxiety
A Myth-Busting Guide

So, when it comes to anxiety, people often have a lot of pre-conceptions and assumptions. Some of these myths are more general to anyone with anxiety, and some are more related to the intersection of being trans and being anxious. These anxiety myths can be something other people tell us, or think, but they can also be things we think as well. Some of them are pretty ingrained into our society, and end up in our heads as a consequence, even if we don't want them to.

A classic example in my case was that if I took medication for my anxiety I was somehow weak, or letting my anxiety win. It was a real problem and stopped me getting help for a considerable amount of time. I'm not sure exactly where this idea came from, or how it got into my head, but it was a thing for me for longer than I'd like.

These preconceptions, or myths, are often quite damaging and are based on stereotypes and generalizations, which isn't really that helpful for any of us. Therefore, in this chapter we're going to take a look at a few of them and break them down a bit.

Let's look at some more general anxiety myths first, followed by others that are related to our transness. Some of these will seem pretty familiar to a lot of us.

General anxiety myths

Anxiety is just something young people/women/other random but specific group of people get

Everyone gets anxious. It isn't limited to an age group, or gender, or anything other than being alive. Some people experience it more than others, but anxiety can't be broken down to just being a young person's thing, for example, any more than saying that being tall is just a man thing.

Anxiety is just a modern thing – back in the old days we all just got on with it

I think the thing to remember here is that in the 'old days' people just didn't really have the words to describe what anxiety was. It wasn't like back then (whenever that was) there was nothing that was stressful or traumatizing or anxiety-inducing. The world has always been a place where anxiety exists; it's just the way we look at it that has changed, and now more people are talking about it.

Also, Hippocrates wants a word.

Most people that say they have anxiety are just trying to be cool because it's cool to have anxiety nowadays

Let's take a step back for a second.

First, there are far easier routes to being cool than developing an anxiety disorder: just get a leather jacket or swear more or be a nice person or something.

Second, you're erasing people's feelings, minimizing their suffering, and just being pretty mean. Don't do that. It's not cool.

Exercise/natural herbs/mindfulness/just chilling out more will cure anxiety

Yes, these things will help, and sometimes these things will help loads. Anxiety, though, is as varied and complex as we are as humans. What works for one person might not work for another, and there is no cure-all for this; you've just got to keep on trying till you find the thing or things that work for you. These things are just a piece of the overall jigsaw that is our anxiety.

If you take meds to help your anxiety, you're weak

If medication works for you, then that's all that matters. It's definitely not weak to take medication to correct an imbalance in your body. Think of it like this... If you have a headache, you'll take painkillers, right? So why is anti-anxiety medication any different?

The easiest/best way to cure anxiety is by controlling your breathing better

Again, this can be very effective but it isn't a magical cure-all. To help tackle anxiety we need a whole range of tools, specific to each one of us. To put it another way, you can't build a house with just a hammer.

Most people just grow out of anxiety – it gets better with time

Generalizations are never that great, and there are a lot of them when it comes to anxiety. When people do grow out of anxiety, it's normally because things have changed for them. Anxiety can affect us at any time. For instance, as a teenager you might have anxiety around exams, but then as a 30-something adult you might have a great job and feel less anxious. This might change again as you get older and start to worry about where you're going to live, or if you develop health problems. Anxiety is circumstantial and related to what's happening to you at that moment in time.

Anxiety and stress are just the same thing

Stress and anxiety are related but they're not really the same. Stress can lead to anxiety, but stress tends to be more of the moment, whilst anxiety tends to stick around for much longer.

Say you're going for a job interview. You'll probably feel a bit stressed about it. If, however, this is your tenth interview and you've got this sneaking suspicion that the reason you're not getting all these jobs is because you're trans, then it's quite likely that the stress you're feeling has developed into full-blown anxiety.

Only weirdos and freaks get anxious – normal/other people are all fine

Ugh! I've heard this one a few times, but basically let's just not do this. Anyone can get anxiety. We are all weird. Don't call people freaks. And, again, anyone can be anxious. There is no normal.

Only introverts/shy people get anxiety – successful people don't get anxiety

Loads of singers, politicians, actors, performers and seemingly outgoing people have anxiety issues. Anxiety can amplify introversion and shyness but it's not limited to introverts and shy people.

Panic attacks can make you pass out

This can happen, but it's not as likely as you might think. Fainting happens when your blood pressure falls dramatically. When you're having a panic attack, your blood pressure normally rises.

The thing that can sometimes cause you to faint is hyperventilation. When you hyperventilate, you breathe in too much oxygen and get rid of too much carbon dioxide too quickly. That narrows your blood vessels and slows blood flow to your brain, which can make you pass out. This is why breathing is so important in helping with attacks. Breath control helps the light-headed, dizzy, fainting feelings that occur, because it stops you from hyperventilating.

Anxiety isn't real/an illness

Anxiety is a natural part of life. Sometimes it can be helpful – it alerts us to danger, for instance – but sometimes it can get out of control.

Anxiety disorders are some of the most common mental illnesses to affect us. They have been researched by experts and can be diagnosed by health care professionals. Research by Hannah Ritchie and Max Roser estimated that 284 million people globally suffer from an anxiety disorder.[1] The true number is likely a lot higher, as stigma and circumstances often prevent people from talking about it and getting a diagnosis.

Only humans get anxiety

I heard someone say this the other day and I thought to myself, 'You've clearly never had a pet.' The person had also clearly never watched any of the videos on YouTube of cats comforting anxious dogs, or the one with the anxious goat that calms down when she wears a duck costume, or the video of the vet who sings songs to his animal patients when they get all anxious.

People with anxiety should always avoid any stressful situations

Good luck with that. I mean, yeah, in an ideal world definitely

---

1 Ritchie, H. and Roser, M. (2018) 'Mental Health.' Available at https://ourworldindata .org/mental-health.

avoid stressful situations, but if we just jump back to Stoicism briefly, a lot of what happens to us in the world is out of our control. What we can control is how we react, which is probably where we should put our focus, maybe?

If you really want to, you can just snap out of your anxiety/ You're just making a fuss for attention

Kinda rude and, again, this is something we hear way too much. It's like people assume we haven't already considered this. What's that? I should just snap out of it? Ooooh, shit! Looks like Sherlock Holmes here just solved the case! Pack it up gang, looks like this book is done.

And I'm not even going to go into the attention thing. Just no. Remember, just because you don't relate to something, it doesn't suddenly make it not real.

Forcing yourself to do things that make you anxious is the only way to overcome them

I mean, it might, but also it might make it worse. For some people this might be a great way to overcome anxiety, and there is a type of therapy that works on this principle, but for others it might be the worst decision ever. Generalizations are our worst enemy sometimes because they don't allow for the nuances and experiences of each person.

Professional help for anxiety, like therapy, is just a con

Talking about things that are bothering you is always important. The trick is finding the right person. A good therapist will change your life, but a bad one will just make it worse. I've been seeing a therapist for over five years now, and for me it's been life-changing – in part, because I have an amazing therapist, but also because I've been seeing them for so long. Therapy can be useful for short-term stuff, but it really shines when it comes to longer-term issues.

People with anxiety will also suffer from other issues like disordered eating, self-harm, addiction, etc.

I think the thing to remember with this is that it's people, rather than just people with anxiety, that can suffer from other issues. We all have stuff going on, and things that we struggle with, and quite often these things can give us anxiety. I think it's easy sometimes to think of anxiety as a cause of something, when in reality anxiety is actually a result of something. For example, I have food-related issues sometimes, so I can be a bit funny about other people touching my food because I worry about cleanliness. I don't have this because of anxiety, but it does cause me anxiety.

Anxiety can be traced back to one bad experience in your past

There is a type of anxiety that is linked to a traumatic experience, or experiences, and that's post-traumatic stress disorder (PTSD). The *Diagnostic and Statistical Manual of Mental Disorders* describes it as exposure to actual or threatened death, serious injury, or sexual violence.[2] This can include things like being in a car crash, having major surgery, and natural disasters or extreme violence being done to yourself or loved ones. It's well documented that these events can create extreme and life-changing levels of anxiety, so yes, anxiety can be traced back to bad experiences in your life.

The thing is, though, anxiety can also happen for any number

---

2   American Psychiatric Association (2013) *Diagnostic and Statistical Manual of Mental Disorders (DSM-5)*. Washington, DC: American Psychiatric Association Publishing.

of reasons, such as your identity, life events, where you live, and so on. Anxiety is complex, and as humans we have a strong need to understand complex things. We also have a strong urge to pin our anxiety on a single cause in order for it to make sense, and become easier to understand.

I know this because for years I've been looking for that one thing to pin my anxiety on. I remember thinking that if only I could find the answer, then I'd have something to go on, something that I could say was the problem.

Of course, there was no *one* thing, and actually, even if there was, I feel like that would be just one more thing in a long list of anxiety-causing things that happen over the course of a lifetime.

You can't be anxious and happy/If you're not anxious all the time you don't have anxiety/Feeling okay sometimes means you don't have anxiety
It's easy to feel that if you have a good feeling it invalidates all the bad things that have happened. We live in a world where we're often told that, where our negative experiences are dismissed or brushed aside as soon as we show any degree of joy in something. The thing is, though, you can still watch a film and have it make you laugh, and then feel anxious an hour later because you get a text message you don't want to respond to.

It's completely valid to feel okay sometimes; and it's important to feel okay sometimes, if only to give yourself a break.

You need to just get over it, to just sort it out, to stop whining because so many other people have got it worse
It sometimes feels like there's a hierarchy of suffering, but, in reality, suffering is relative to each person experiencing it.

Now, obviously there are definitely some things that are

worse than other things, but that doesn't mean that the lesser things are any less valid to the person experiencing them.

Someone who is sitting in a dark room and can't stop shaking because their anxiety is overwhelming them so much is having a pretty awful time of it. Other people may well have it worse, but that doesn't mean that suddenly your stuff is invalid. That's not how suffering and pain work.

Trans-specific myths

A lot of the things we've spoken about so far are pretty universal, but let's take a closer look at some of the things that specifically affect us as trans people. Again, these are things that people have said to me, as well as things that I've had pop into my head.

Having gender reassignment surgery/facial feminization surgery will cure my anxiety

So yeah, it probably will help, but only if it's something you want. Not every trans person will have surgery, and not every trans person will want surgery.

There's sometimes quite a bit of pressure within our community over surgeries. I can remember early on in my transition getting asked by both cis and other trans people when I'd be having my op. When I replied that I wasn't sure if it was the right thing for me at that moment, it regularly caused consternation and confusion.

As humans we have a tendency to think that if something has worked for us, it'll also work for everybody else, especially if we perceive that person as being like us. For me, having facial feminization surgery (FFS) was really important, and once I finally did that, it definitely helped with my anxiety, especially in relation to my own self-worth, and identity. It made me feel more complete and whole within my body, which lessened my anxiety.

However, this is just how it was for me. It would be impossible for me to know that this would be the same for everyone, because we are all different and have different experiences. Sharing personal experiences is important and can be very helpful. It's what helped me decide that FFS was right for me, but I had to reach that decision on my own terms, not by being told that this was the only way.

I'm only anxious because I'm trans/ All trans people are anxious

Well, I mean, you're not entirely wrong there. Being trans does come with a big spoonful of anxiety. Remember when we talked earlier about anxiety being a result of something? Well, although anxiety and transness are linked, the anxiety is often more the result of how the rest of the world treats us as trans people.

Again, we're dealing with some pretty big generalizations here as well. It's like saying all people are always anxious, forgetting, of course, that anxiety isn't a constant state of being. It ebbs and flows; sometimes we're more anxious than at other times, and sometimes we're actually fine, thank you. As trans people, we experience anxiety, and it could be said that we're more likely to experience it as well, but you can't just say we are all anxious, because it's not going to be the case for everyone.

Trans people are difficult/impossible to be with because they're all anxious

I've had this thrown at me quite a few times now, combined with the more general 'Trans people are a hot mess, so avoid them like the plague.' I mean, yes, if you have anxiety, then sometimes that's going to be difficult to deal with for other people, but who doesn't have stuff that's difficult to deal with sometimes?

We're all a little messy, complex and have emotional baggage. Some of that stuff can make relationships tricky; but equally, any relationship with another person is always going to have things that are more complicated.

I guess it's about what works for you, and what you can manage. If you're not dating trans people because they're anxious, then I guess you're just not dating anyone else either because... Surprise! It's not just trans people that get anxiety.

Trans women are more anxious than trans men

Again, it's not that simple. This actually comes from a pretty unpleasant place as well, as it plays into the myth that trans men have it easier than trans women.

What's actually the case is that trans people all face different challenges, based on a whole variety of different factors, including things like class, wealth, body shape, identity, ethnicity, if you have a disability or not, and so on. There are a lot of different factors involved in the anxiety each different person experiences, based on the many intersections of who they are.

Because there's a preconception that trans men pass better, even though this actually isn't true for everyone, it's assumed that trans men will experience less that will trigger anxiety, because so much of trans women's anxiety is caused by cis people reading them as trans and hating it.

Coming out/fully transitioning will help with my anxiety

This is so much about us all as individuals. For some of us, coming out might make our situation worse, as we might be somewhere unsafe, whilst for others it might well be really empowering. For me, coming out and transitioning did help with my anxiety. It didn't make it go away, though. I still get anxiety, so it's important to recognize that, like so many other things, coming out can help but it's not everything.

Anxiety medication will interfere with my hormone medication

It's always best to check with your doctor if you feel concerned about anything related to health. For people taking oestrogen as hormone replacement therapy (HRT), studies suggest that anxiety medication shouldn't interfere with it, and that being on HRT can actually sometimes reduce anxiety symptoms.[3]

With testosterone replacement, research has shown that testosterone can help bind antidepressants in the brain, potentially making them more effective.[4] When researching this I did also find some reports of people experiencing lower testosterone levels when taking antidepressants, but this was all anecdotal, and not backed up by any empirical research as far as I could see. If you feel in any way concerned about your hormone levels though, do check with your doctor.

Personally, I've taken anti-anxiety medication whilst having oestrogen replacement medication, and it's been okay. But I repeat, *always check with a doctor.*

These are just a few of the many myths and preconceptions that exist around anxiety, but there are many more besides. It's important to try and debunk these myths as much as possible, as they don't help anyone and never show us the full picture. We

---

3   White Hughto, J.M. and Reisner, S.L. (2016) 'A systematic review of the effects of hormone therapy on psychological functioning and quality of life in transgender individuals.' *Transgender Health* 1, 1, 21–31.

4   Kranz, G.S., Wadsak, W., Kaufmann, U., Salvi, M. *et al.* (2015) 'High-dose testosterone treatment increases serotonin transporter binding in transgender people.' *Biological Psychiatry* 78, 525–533.

often like to try and simplify things, and often stuff gets treated as fact without any checking to see if it actually is.

Sometimes the things we hear and take in are only part of what's going on, and touting just one thing as the cure-all for anxiety can be really detrimental if you try that thing and it doesn't work.

Hopefully, this chapter will have helped clear up some of these myths and made the waters a little less muddy as we all embark on our journey to a more anxiety-free life!

On Anxiety – Sabah

What do you do to feel better when you're feeling anxious?
I exercise a few times a week. It's usually at a time when I just need to get out of the house, away from a conversation or screen that's stressing me out. I didn't realize it until recently but exercising felt great whilst anxious because the physiological effects on my body, heart racing, sweating, etc. are the same. I don't know how to explain it, but heart racing/sweating from exercise felt better than from anxiety. My anxiety was distracted, and I could pinpoint a reason for these physical feelings, when it's not always easy to find a reason for anxiety in my body.

I try to quickly accept it, so then I can just draw a line under whatever task/activity I am in the middle of doing and just move on. Cross it out. It's done for right now. Try again in a few hours/tomorrow/next week. Not failed. Just, I'm done with it now and I'm moving on to either feel better or try something else – no point staying here whilst I'm anxious, because I know how this ends and it doesn't get better.

I sit with myself and write a list of all the commitments I have, starting with work, to family and friends, to personal health and wellbeing. I write timelines or deadlines where I can. And then I try to prioritize what I need to do, what I have to do, and what I can cancel or ask someone else to do. It isn't easy, because it can often stress how much depends on me, but sometimes, it makes me see: 'I really don't have to be at this meeting, I can catch up,' for work; or 'Why am I doing this? Do I even want to do this?' for social activities; or 'I don't have to do this. Someone else can do this,' for freelance jobs.

I end up writing similar scribbly lists every day, but just to keep myself focused. When I can see it on paper, it feels manageable if it is little. And if it's big, it validates the stress and pressure I do feel.

If you had one piece of advice for another trans/non-binary person who's experiencing anxiety, what would it be?

Something I've been doing with trans youth I work with is to create a 'dysphoria first-aid kit', which could be a physical box or a drawing of one. Inside we put items and reminders to help our anxiety around gender dysphoria alleviate. Most of it is distraction and comfort, but in those high-anxiety times it's hard to think of anything else that could possibly help.

Whatever you call them – anti-anxiety remedies, self-care plans – they all need attention and revisiting. Our anxiety changes as we do – especially as we change genders, bodies, expressions, our anxiety transitions just like us. If our needs change, our remedies change too. A self-care plan is not a forever plan, so don't expect it to always work. When it doesn't work, you are not failing. You're learning something new about yourself; your needs are just different now and it's time to try something else. Being active in our own care and recovery is just as important as investing in it.

How does being trans/non-binary affect your anxiety?
When I was binding my chest, it restricted my breathing and chest in subtle ways that would just build over the day, and I'd feel really anxious without knowing why. I remember one time I started to have an anxiety attack when I was out with friends in a pub. Suddenly I just had to move, navigate a really busy pub and gendered toilets to just lock myself in a cubicle, take off my t-shirt and binder and just stand there topless, gasping. I don't know how long I was there for, but I was so confused, upset, dysphoric, worried... Everything was going through my head. And I couldn't really explain it to the cis friends I was with. It's mostly physical, but the physical has so much weight for gender-nonconforming bodies. It becomes mental and emotional so quickly, without us even realizing. All these parts of our experience are so connected.

CHAPTER 2

Can I Fix My Anxiety?

It's important for us all to know that anxiety can get better over time. Here's the rub, though: it can only get better if we do something about it, which is often hard or near impossible because of, well, anxiety. It's a vicious circle, in that you make the decision that you don't want to feel like this any more, but then when you try to do anything about it, you just get overwhelmed by anxiety, which is the actual thing you're trying to do something about in the first place, because you don't want to feel like this any more.

It sucks.

Here's an example. Part of my recovery from my anxious self was to get some therapy. It makes sense, it's a proven way of managing and understanding difficult things and I know it works for me. So, I just needed to go out and get some. Sounds easy, right? Yeah... Nope.

First off, although I really needed to see someone, I also really didn't want to. I didn't want to open up to a stranger about my stuff, I didn't want to share, and anyhow I was actually fine most of the time. Or rather I thought I was fine most of the time.

Truthfully, I was a mess. It took a close friend to point this out. And two screaming arguments with other friends over the most stupid shit that really didn't matter. Oh, and the realization that I was constantly bursting into tears from stress, anxiety and sadness, even though the story in my head was basically 'It's all fine, I'm all fine.'

Even then, once I began to consider therapy, there were still the age-old worries that we often all face as trans people: Will the person I see be trans inclusive? Will they even know what trans is? Am I just going to spend all my therapy sessions explaining this? Are they just going to assume everything that's messed up about me is because I'm trans? Is my trans identity going to dominate this to the point where the therapy doesn't actually help at all? Is this a good choice?

Thankfully for me, it was, but it easily could have gone the other way. It's always a risk when you're trans. I guess that's part of it. In order to actually do something about your anxiety, you're going to have to take risks. For us as trans people, those risks feel pretty extreme sometimes, which isn't to belittle other non-trans people's experiences at all – anyone considering doing something about their anxiety is taking a risk. It's all risky. It's just that sometimes some of us face more risks than others, depending on our identity and its intersections, especially in relation to privilege and oppressions.

Privileges, oppressions and anxiety

When we think about how we can tackle our anxiety, it's helpful to also think about our privilege and our oppressions and how they can affect things.

Privilege is a word that comes up more and more in our world, especially in relation to talking about activism and social justice.

In the context of anxiety, though, we're going to talk about how it affects how we feel, and what limitations or advantages it can give us.

So what is privilege exactly? Well, it was first spoken about by W.E.B. Du Bois, back in the 1930s, who wrote about the 'psychological wage' that allowed white people to feel superior to black people.[1] This idea of aspects of who you are giving you an advantage, or benefit, especially in relation to unearned or unacknowledged benefits, was fleshed out in the 1980s by Peggy McIntosh, who wrote *White Privilege and Male Privilege: A Personal Account of Coming to See Correspondences through Work in Women's Studies*.[2] Examples of privilege that I have, for example, are that I'm white, I'm middle class, I'm employed, I'm non-disabled, and I'm thin. These things all make my life a bit easier.

Examples of oppressions (the opposite of privilege) I have, or experience, would be that I'm trans, I'm a woman and I have PTSD. As a white, middle-class woman who has a job, I'm more able to access things like therapy because I can afford the cost. As a white person, systemic racism isn't going to affect me in the way it would a person of colour, so it's going to be that much easier to find a good therapist. This isn't to say that a black person isn't going to be able to find a good therapist if they want one; just that they're more likely to run into issues like gatekeeping, appropriation and roadblocking, because of our society's systemic racism. As a trans woman, though, I might find it difficult to actually find a therapist who understands the issues I'm coming with, because I know from experience that

---

1   Du Bois, W.E.B. (1935) 'Back Toward Slavery.' *Black Reconstruction in America 1860–1880.* San Diego, CA: Harcourt.

2   McIntosh, P. (1988) *White Privilege and Male Privilege: A Personal Account of Coming to See Correspondences through Work in Women's Studies* (Working Paper 189). Wellesley, MA: Wellesley Centers for Women. Available at https://nationalseedproject.org/Key-SEED-Texts/white-privilege-and-male-privilege.

a lot of people have difficulties or issues with understanding trans identities.

This is important to understand, because sometimes it can feel like your privileges can negate or erase your oppressions. This can lead to more anxiety, and feelings of worthlessness, like your issues aren't as important or real as other people's.

It's good to remember that we don't experience our privileges and oppressions separately – they're all interlinked and part of our whole. These interactions are called 'intersections', and this is where the term 'intersectionality' (a word coined by Kimberlé Crenshaw, who used it to talk about the experiences of black women[3]) comes from. To give an example, as a woman I experience sexism and misogyny. All women experience this in some shape or form, but as a visible trans woman there's also another layer to this for me, as the sexism I experience can also be informed by transphobia and homophobia. This doesn't make what I experience more important than the sexism a cis woman experiences, but it does make it harder.

In relation to anxiety, our privileges and oppressions can make getting help more complex, especially as our oppressions by their very nature can disempower us, both in our real-world interactions and our mental states.

As I mentioned before, if you're employed and earning a wage, it might make it easier to access paid services like therapy or medical care. If you're poor or on a low income, then these things might well be beyond your reach. You might try to get work to enable you to afford these things, but other aspects of who you are might make this harder to achieve. As a trans person, for

---

3   Crenshaw, K. (1989) 'Demarginalizing the Intersection of Race and Sex: A Black Feminist Critique of Antidiscrimination Doctrine, Feminist Theory and Antiracist Politics.' University of Chicago Legal Forum: Vol. 1989: Iss. 1, Article 8. Available at http://chicagounbound.uchicago.edu/uclf/vol1989/iss1/8.

instance, it's much harder to get work because trans people are discriminated against. Although I have a job now, it took me a long time to find one, and I ended up working in the charity sector because that was more well known for tolerance and acceptance of minorities.

It's tough sometimes because it's easy to get caught up in your oppressions and privileges – they can become consuming and act as a barrier, both in the real world and in your head.

Anxiety can really do a number on this as well. It can make all our efforts seem pointless, and it becomes easy to label our oppressions as being the reason why we can't do something. This isn't to say that this isn't the case – we know that our oppressions can make it harder to do the things we want and need – but it can also be helpful to know that our oppressions can be like fuel for our anxiety. Getting past the anxiety that's informed by our oppressions can be a rough ride because the very nature of oppression is, well, to be oppressive.

It's easy to feel like you have no options and that any future you have is limited, and stifled. The thing is, though, this isn't exactly true. We often get stuck because things are just really, really hard. Because your options are limited by your oppressions, it can feel like there's nowhere to go, but there are nearly always options, even if they're not the options you necessarily want. Sometimes, if something is incredibly difficult to do, it can seem hopeless, but it's worth stepping back for a moment and trying to see more of the picture. When you're in the thick of it, this may seem like an impossible thing to do, so you need to remove yourself from what's going on as much as possible.

Find a space where you can think, a space that's distraction-free and, most importantly, stress/anxiety-free, and start working things out. Going back for a moment to the example of being able to afford health care (something we'll go into more detail on in Chapter 8), let's break it down a bit. You want to have some surgery, as you know it will help relieve a lot of the anxiety you feel around your body. Surgery, if you go through private healthcare, or need something the NHS doesn't offer, costs money though – lots of money, which you don't have. This feeds your anxiety because you can't see a way you'll ever be able to afford this, making the whole situation start to feel hopeless. You still want this surgery, but you don't have a way to access it, which creates more anxiety on top of what you're already experiencing. It's easy to see how this can become a downward spiral, so we need to stop for a moment and try and work out where to break the circle.

Things that are facts right now are:

1. You need this surgery.

2. You can't afford it.

These two statements tend to be the ones our anxious brains fixate on. There are, however, some addendums that are also true that we can add to these two statements.

a. You need this surgery – at some point in your life.

b. You can't afford it – yet.

These two statements are also still true, but they give a slightly wider angle to work with. Obviously, they're not ideal; you really want to be able to afford the surgery right now, but that's just not possible at the moment, so instead we have to work with what we have.

So, let's look at what we have now and put some boundaries

and goals around this. We've established we need this surgery but that we can't afford it. Those are facts. But let's expand on this a bit more with some questions that'll help us reach this goal:

- How long am I prepared to wait to get this surgery?

- How much do I really want this?

- How much time is it going to take to be able to afford it?

- What other information do I need in order to do this?

- What ways can I use to raise money?

- What are my privileges, and my oppressions, and how might they affect what I'd like to achieve?

- Are there any other options I can look at, both long and short term?

- What are my limits?

- How can I look after myself while I work out a way to do this?

It's important to be realistic in answering these sorts of questions and to be aware of the privileges and oppressions you have that may help or hinder your progress, because this can help give you a roadmap to your final goal. Everyone will have a different map, because we are all unique, and all have different intersections within our identity.

Taking the above example of surgery, here's my own experience. I wanted some FFS but couldn't afford it, so I worked through some of these questions to try and help me achieve what I wanted, with the least stress and anxiety.

How long am I prepared to wait to get this surgery?
As long as it takes. I accepted that it was going to take a long time. It was shit having to accept this, and it did make me very depressed and anxious at times; but, equally, knowing that I would do this, even if it meant waiting years, also gave me some hope. (In the end it took nearly six years, timed from when I decided that I wanted this surgery, to actually having it.)

What ways can I use to raise money?
I considered a lot of options. These included:

- crowdfunding

- borrowing/loans

- saving

- getting extra work/whatever work I could

- asking friends and family to help out

- sex work

- selling all my stuff.

There are many options, but not all of them are options for everyone. I decided against sex work and crowdfunding, for example, because although there was the potential for earning more money, my anxiety was too extreme when it came to both those things. These were my limits, which did mean that it took more time, but it also meant that I felt less stress and anxiety.

What are my privileges, and my oppressions, and how might they affect what I'd like to achieve?
My transness is something that can be used to oppress me, so

I need to be aware of that, and work out ways to offset the oppression as much as possible.

For example, travelling through airports (to access where I wanted to go for my surgery) can be difficult as a trans person, especially if you're asked to use the full-body scanners (these can sometimes flag up parts of your body if you haven't had particular surgeries, outing you or worse). As a white person, I also know that it's less likely to develop into something serious if I do get flagged up going through airport security.

Accessing medical care can also be more complex if the people delivering it are not aware of trans people or have misconceptions about us.

To help lessen the anxiety around all this I chose to have someone I trust come with me (for support and to be able to step in if there was a problem), and I chose a hospital and surgeons that had a proven track record of working with trans people.

What other information do I need in order to do this?
I did a lot of research. I read first-hand accounts, got costing quotes, asked people who'd had surgeries what it was like, looked at the different places I could go to have my surgery, and so much more. I got as much information as I could find, so I knew exactly what I needed to do.

Being informed helped me with working out what was realistic for me as well. I knew that if the surgery was going to cost £60,000, for instance, then that might be difficult to raise, so I would need to change my expectations accordingly. (It didn't cost this much, but it felt important to me to work out what I could afford, and what I could get for that.)

Again, this is all about setting your limits. I went abroad to have my surgery, but I only went to Spain because, for me, going further afield was too anxiety-inducing. Spain worked for me because I understand basic Spanish, and the person who was coming with me was fluent. We both knew the country really well, and the cost for my surgery at this particular clinic fitted what I could afford, so it ticked most of the boxes I needed to be ticked.

Working out what you can manage – be that in terms of location, cost or mental health, for example – helps make your roadmap clearer, and a clearer roadmap means less anxiety when it comes to finding your way to where you need to be.

How can I look after myself while I work out a way to do this?
This is perhaps one of the most important things you can ask yourself. Make no mistake, this can be a stressful and anxiety-inducing process, so you need to have some mechanisms in place to help.

Going back to limits, it's good to recognize when you've reached yours. I had to recognize that this was going to take time. I wanted to get this all sorted as quickly as I could, but in reality this just wasn't going to happen quickly.

If things got too overwhelming for me because of this, I'd try and remember to use coping techniques I'd developed – things like going for a walk or doing something to distract myself. I'd try and talk to others about it, to share the load and lessen the anxiety I was feeling. Sometimes I just had a really big cry.

It's vital that you find a way (or ways) to look after yourself. Without mechanisms to do this, whatever goal you're trying to reach will feel more and more unobtainable, and you'll get stuck in that vicious circle of wanting this thing but not being able to get it.

Of course, it's worth saying again that this is my experience, and other people, in different situations, may have a very different ride to the one I had. This isn't meant to be a universal solution, because there is no universal solution, but rather a way forward that might be a helpful starting point to dealing with anxiety.

We started this section talking about privilege, so let's go back to that again. Your privileges and oppressions give you various advantages and disadvantages in life. They can give you perspectives on life that others may not have, even if they can also be limiting for you personally. As a trans person it can sometimes feel like all we have is oppression, especially in today's world, and this can really increase anxiety levels. The thing is, though, we do have options and choices, even if they're not always the ones we'd really like.

It might feel like the only options you have are all bad and there's no way out, but it's still worth exploring those options because bad short term might well lead to good long term.

Resilience

Life can be pretty hard sometimes, right? I think that's something most of us can relate to in some shape or form.

You'll often hear people talking about resilience, and how it's super-helpful in surviving all the things that life throws at you; but what exactly does that mean, and how can it help with anxiety?

Resilience is about how well we deal with difficult things. The Finns have a word, 'sisu', which is often used to describe a sense of grit, resolve, or stoic tenacity, especially in the face of adversity or difficult odds.

Sisu basically describes resilience. It's about how we manage and adapt in tricky times.

The best thing about resilience is that you probably already have some. Our world is constantly changing, and it can get really overwhelming, especially for us as trans people. Our personal resilience is what gets us through all this.

Our resilience is part of what we use to enable transition, especially if it's in the face of adversity (which, let's face it, is often the case). Resilience is that feeling of not giving up despite the odds. It's trying to find a realistic positive in a bad situation and persisting in what you want for your future. It's about thinking big, and pushing forwards, trying your best to make the changes you might face – your changes, rather than ones that are put upon you. Resilience is what keeps us all going.

Resilience doesn't make problems or uncertainties go away. It doesn't make stress or anxiety a thing of the past or stop you feeling these things. What it does do is allow you to recover from these things and stay positive. Resilience lets you carry on despite all this, and not only carry on, but also thrive and grow stronger from it.

The great thing about resilience is that it's something that develops and becomes stronger and stronger as well, mainly because it helps you push through the things that limit you in getting what you need and want. Like a muscle, the more you use it, the stronger it gets. Every time we use our resilience to push through something that feels like an obstacle in our path, we also learn that we have the power to change difficult things.

How do we actually build resilience? Well, resilience is something you can get through other people. Having a strong support network of friends, family or loved ones can really help. Your network can also offer help and advice as well as support, so it can also include people such as GPs or mental health support workers. Having a connected, supportive network of people gives you back-up resilience to support what you already have within yourself.

Resilience also builds up when you take care of yourself. Think of it like an energy bar in a video game. If you're constantly under attack, then it's going to go down, so you're going to need to recharge it at some point! You can do this by being kind to yourself. Do things you enjoy, eat nice food, get a good night's sleep, hang out with friends, or try and practise some stress management techniques like yoga or meditation. Being kind to yourself is a powerful thing. It's a way of giving yourself a break and catching your breath. It can also add meaning to life, which can add to your resilience. If things are meaningful, then they become worth fighting for, they become something that matters; and when something matters, then you also develop resilience.

It can help as well if you try to be as proactive as possible. When we face setbacks, it can drain our resilience and feel like it's just one thing after another. It can help sometimes to try and step back and see what you can do to try and make things better by making a plan, for example (much like we spoke about earlier on).

Sometimes it can be helpful to look back on past experiences and see if there's anything you can learn from them. The fact that you've got through hard times before shows that you do have resilience and skills to help you navigate difficult situations, even if it doesn't feel like it at the time.

Having resilience is a really useful tool in tackling anxiety because it will enable you to persevere, and to carry on, even when things are tough. It's like an extra armour-coating for your life, and that feels like something we could all find useful at times.

On Anxiety – Eris

What does anxiety look and feel like for you?

Anxiety for me was (I've thankfully not experienced it in a while) always a 'gut feeling', like a clenching panic or unrest in my gut that I would carry around with me in my day-to-day while doing other things. It would also manifest as fear of certain situations like talking on the phone, doing 'admin' like filling out tax forms (I cried in the university tax office when I went in to file for my first job as an undergrad!), and it always felt really organic, as if it was an intrinsic part of me, or part of life in general.

What do you do to feel better when you're feeling anxious?

Nowadays I can instantly distinguish between anxiety and general nervousness, and I haven't had to deal with proper anxiety very much in the last few years. Anxiety and depression (which went hand in hand for me) also really tended to do a number on my memory, so a lot of the time I was mentally ill is kind of just missing from my memory! So, it's a bit hard to remember what I did in the moment to feel better. I think being able to distance myself when possible, to get away from situations that were causing my fear and anxiety and into a place where I didn't have to 'pretend' to be healthy, helped. I had safe living circumstances and liked my roommates, some of whom were going through these things as well. Understanding I wasn't the only person going through it helped a lot. So did recognizing that I was experiencing mental illness; and getting over my shame and reaching out to people like counsellors and my mother for help or to let them know I was struggling, was really difficult but helped too.

If you had one piece of advice for another trans/non-binary person who's experiencing anxiety, what would it be?

I've only rarely experienced true anxiety in the last few years, thanks to having gone through CBT [cognitive behavioural therapy] at my undergrad university health office, and having transitioned.

Sometimes anxiety is caused by brain chemicals (or whatever the science says now), and sometimes it's caused by an untenable life situation or other external cause, and sometimes (a lot I think!) it's a combination of both. Sometimes anxiety manifests in one area of life, when the cause of anxiety is in another. Look at your life and be honest: are there parts of your life that are unsustainable?

For me it was not transitioning, and staying in my current relationship, which wasn't healthy for me or my partner. Transitioning and breaking up were hard – like really difficult. When I think back they were probably two of the most difficult things I had done at that point in my life, and they both filled me with fear. But when I realized that I couldn't sustain the way I was living, and was forced to do something to change my life, it made me realize I could have some control over my life and do things even if they require hard work, and that knowledge has served me well ever since. Hard work is good! What's the point of life if you don't have to do difficult things?

The other piece of advice I'd give people, then, is to seek therapy if you can, especially LGBTQ+ – and *especially* non-binary-friendly therapy, if at all possible. Try online/video chat therapy! CBT isn't for everyone but it totally rewired my brain – it worked like magic: I can't even remember a single thing my therapist said – it just worked. And ask your therapist about medication, too. I think the stigma against taking necessary anti-anxiety meds (or other mental illness treatments) is start-ing to go away, but still holds in some circles. But if you need it, you need it! And there's nothing wrong with that.

What one thing, above all others, helps you when it comes to your anxiety?
I think for me a lot of anxiety comes/came from fear of things I had, or thought I had, no control over. So, allowing myself to set aside things that I can't control and that I don't need to engage with (like reading the news during the coronavirus pandemic), and to prioritize the things I can, gives me a feeling of control over my own life and my own future, which is fundamentally different from how I felt when I was dealing with anxiety.

How does being trans/non-binary affect your anxiety?
The #1 way it affected it is that one thing I realized when anxiety became too much to bear was that I *needed* to transition. I just couldn't not. Coming out as non-binary, even to myself, made a huge difference – and ties in with that need for a semblance of control over my own life.

CHAPTER 3

Anxiety and Other Emotions

So, when I get anxious, what happens? I know, of course, that there's all the science stuff about neural pathways, and the amygdala and hippocampus getting all feisty and riled up, but what actually does anxiety do to me? How does it make me behave? What's going on there?

These are big questions that are often hard to answer, especially while you're in the throes of an anxiety attack. In that moment your mind is so preoccupied with the actual anxiety, it's virtually impossible to be able to stop and see what's happening.

Something that can be very helpful in breaking this down is a thing called a 'feelings wheel'. There are loads out there on the internet and they help you discover what's really going on with the emotions you're feeling. For example, feeling overwhelmed can be a sign of anxiety, which in turn can be simplified as feeling fearful or afraid.

Over time, I've started noticing some of the things I do and ways I behave, and how they break down, especially in relation to anxiety. Obviously, this is just my own experience, but having said that, I think there's also a lot of common ground here, and certainly I've found it super-helpful to learn about what I do and how I behave when I'm feeling anxious. I think of the emotions and feelings described below as a sort of early warning system now, letting me know that something is amiss, and that sneaky anxiety is creeping in, looking for a way to mess up my day.

Anger

This is something I've only recently realized, and I think that's because, honestly, there's a lot that makes me a bit narky and irritable. When there's something that you feel quite a lot already, it's sometimes very hard to separate it out and break it down.

Here's an example. When I'm not writing books, I work in an office doing admin-type stuff. Anyone who has ever worked in admin will know that there's a lot within that role that will try your patience and, yes, make you quite irritable. Anyhow, a while back, my boss asked me to go on some training, which to all intents and purposes seems pretty reasonable. There was a load of new legislation coming into law about data protection, and someone needed to learn about it, and that someone was going to be me.

And, yep, you've guessed it. I was so cross about having to go on this course. Like irrationally angry and irritated about it. In my diary, on the date the course was going to be, I'd written:

Data Protection BLAH BLAH STUPID COURSE WHY?

In capitals.

I think we can all agree that's pretty angry.

On the surface, me going on this course was entirely reasonable. I dealt with a lot of our data, so it obviously needed to be me. I'd get my travel costs and time paid for. There was even a hot lunch provided, which anyone who's been on these sorts of things will know is like gold dust in these times of austerity.

What's not to love?

Why am I being such an asshole about this seemingly reasonable request?

The short answer, of course, is anxiety. It's what this book is all about, so really it would be weird if it wasn't that in this context.

Once I started to break it down and look into why anxiety was making me feel this rage, I also started to see what was really going on.

I was feeling angry, and by association anxious, because I was having to do something I clearly didn't want to do. But what was it exactly I didn't want to do?

Well, first, the course was in a different city to the one I live in. This meant going somewhere new, with new situations, new rules, and new, potentially more challenging, ways I was going to have to navigate the world. As a trans person this can be pretty difficult.

Where I live I know where it's safe to walk. I know the quickest routes from A to B and I feel streetwise enough within my local area to avoid any situations that might arise. By this I mean I know how best to avoid potential transphobia and street abuse. That's not to say it doesn't happen, it's just that I'm better equipped to deal with it in a familiar area. I can get to a safe place because I know where I am.

In a different city that all goes out the window, especially if I'm going somewhere new. This makes me anxious because I'm worried about my safety and what I'm going to do if something happens. It's worth pointing out here as well that even if nothing happens I'm still going to be feeling this. Anxiety is about perceived threat, and it doesn't really matter how likely that threat is.

In reality, I don't get harassed or face transphobia every single time I go somewhere new, but when it has happened it's been extreme enough for me to now feel anxiety around this. Looking at it from an evolutionary perspective, it makes sense as well. If we experience a dangerous or threatening situation, it makes sense to be hypervigilant about it happening again, if only to protect us. Unfortunately, this sometimes gets skewed. Because I've experienced transphobic attacks, my brain has made the leap that this will always happen in new places. The thought of going somewhere different links up with the 'bad things that happen in new places' bit of my brain and, boom, hello anxiety.

The other thing I don't want to do is also about the new, though this time it's about meeting new people. Back for its regular slot, it's our old pal social anxiety!

Social anxiety is pretty common. Most people experience it in some shape or form, and we'll talk about this later in the book as well. Basically, for a lot of us trans people, social anxiety is like a constant companion.

The thought of meeting new people fills me with absolute dread, and a lot of it is to do with me being trans. Every time I meet someone new, it's a constant guessing game for me as to how they'll react. I've got no idea how they feel about trans people or if they've even met one of us before. I don't know whether they might be a hater or an ally. Sometimes I don't even know if they've realized I'm trans. Honestly, it's a minefield. Again, because I've been in negative situations when it comes to new people and me being trans, my brain has put this all in the threat box and linked it up with anxiety.

It's got to the point now where I can see when people realize or when they just don't get it. I remember being out with some friends a few years ago and a new person (a friend of a friend type situation) joined our group. Introductions were made, and when it got to me I could see he just didn't understand. His face literally screwed up as he tried to compute my name with how he saw me. He even started to say, 'But isn't that a girl's na–' before one of my friends stepped in and dragged him off for a brief Trans 101. When he came back, I could see he still didn't get it. There was that little smirk every time he looked at me, that over-pronouncing of my name and 'accidental' misgendering, that overly aggressive manly attempt to shake my hand like it had all been a misunderstanding, like he was saying, 'Yeah, I hear what I've been told, but I know what you really are.' New people equals attack, and more specifically attack on my trans identity, which is an attack on me, and so again, hello anxiety.

All this anxiety gets turned into anger and frustration, because all this stuff triggers feelings of being attacked, of not being respected, and of not being in control. It could go in any number of ways. Some people might feel hurt or sad, some magical people might even just feel amusement, in a 'whatever' type way, but I know that for me and a lot of others it's anger that comes to the forefront.

Anger in relation to anxiety for me is very much to do with suppression. I've never seen myself as an angry person, despite having a lot of anger within me. As a child I saw anger as being a bad thing, and the self-hatred I've felt has been partly because any anger I've felt has got turned inwards, as I didn't have a healthy way to release it.

My angry reaction to going on a course, for example, was definitely inappropriate and disproportional in relation to what was basically just a new situation. The anger I felt was just a symptom, and when we look beneath that, it starts to become clear that we're actually talking about anxiety.

The anger was a way to try and control a situation that I didn't want to be in, to try and protect me from the things that I know will cause me anxiety. If I get angry, then maybe I won't have to do the thing that's actually deep down making me anxious.

Once we understand that, then it becomes easier to do something about it, which is where a thing called helpful or balanced thinking comes in. It's not easy, but with a bit of practice it can help a lot. Let's take me going on a course as an example:

> I feel angry about going on this course, and when I look into it some more, I find out that the anger I'm feeling is just a symptom of underlying anxiety.

> The anxiety is because I feel worried about how people will react to my transness. (That's putting it in the simplest terms. I know it's more complex than that.)

> Here's what my brain is telling me: DANGER! The world and other people are not safe; they will hurt you. Remember that time in the pub? There's the proof!

Now here's where the helpful thinking comes in. In order to really see the full picture, I need to stop focusing on the bad, and start looking in a more balanced way. Yes, I have experienced bad times to do with my transness, from other people, in other places, but also there've been lots of times where I haven't experienced bad times when I've met new people in other places. The place I'm going to for this course is in a busy part of town, it's on during the daytime and it's facilitated. The people coming to the course are in the same sector as me, so I know they're most likely going to be good people. Once I start looking at the reality of the situation, it starts to seem more and more likely that I'll be okay, and that I don't need to feel anxious, and, by association, angry about this.

It may feel like something awful might happen, but that view is often skewed in favour of keeping us safe, even when it's disproportional to the actual threat. Like so many other things, having a moment to try and think clearly about what's actually going on can really help. It's not so much about coping with the anxiety you're feeling, but rather about understanding what's happening, and how we can connect with our anxiety before any other symptoms, like anger, fear or sadness, get involved. It's only then that we can start to address it head-on and make the changes we need.

I know that for us as trans people the threat is real. We do get attacked, verbally abused, and threatened. For a lot of us this is a reality, but by learning which situations are ones where our threat levels are right to be heightened, and which ones are not, we're actually helping ourselves to become better attuned to who we are and how we work.

Sadness

Feeling sad is a funny thing. Not funny haha, obviously – that's like the exact opposite of sadness. No, I mean it's strange funny. We all have feelings of sadness, but sometimes sadness and anxiety, despite being quite different things, can get really entwined together.

Sadness is often about a sense of loss, something a lot of us are quite familiar with as trans people. We have a lot to grieve for: our lost childhoods, the brutal murders of trans people across the globe, the suicides, the broken relationships, the lost families. Sometimes the list feels endless. When we start to think about all these things, it's hard to not also feel anxious, as everything feels so overwhelming and full-on. The world feels dangerous, which leads to anxiety about everything. Trying to then function within this world becomes increasingly difficult.

Feeling like you've got to keep on holding it together can make you anxious and sad, especially if you also then see everyone else seemingly just going about their day, oblivious to it all. The sense of loss, of feeling like other people will never really know what you're going through, can be extremely intense, and the sadness that comes with this can also be very anxiety-inducing, as it often feels like this will never go away and that this sense of loss is never-ending.

Trying to separate out these feelings can be incredibly helpful. Like with anger, understanding what's really going on can also help with any anxiety you might be feeling. For example, I have what I can only describe as a deep and painful sadness about what my life would have been like if I'd been born cis. This doesn't mean I hate my trans identity – far from it – but I do still have this deep loss about what might have been if things had been different. The sadness I feel about this is sometimes overwhelming, and it hurts me in part because it's something that I have no control over. I can't change anything about it because the past is set in stone.

I remember talking to a friend about this once, and she told me how when she thought about it she could completely see my alternative cis self as married with a load of kids living on a farm. She didn't even need to think about it; it just seemed like the obvious answer to her, and once she'd said it, it felt like an obvious answer to me as well. I could see that version of me.

The anxiety I feel over this sadness is complex and multi-layered. I feel anxious about having a part of me that wishes it were true – that is, the act of wishing sometimes that I wasn't trans feels like a betrayal of my trans identity, and also other people's trans identity. I feel anxious about thinking it and putting it down here, because it feels like I'm letting myself and others down.

There's a sadness as well around our expectations of what we might be. When it comes to hormones especially, there's this narrative that they'll change everything. If you start on testosterone, for example, a common narrative is that you'll get buff really quickly, facial hair will start sprouting like an over-eager forest and your voice will drop like a rock. If you take oestrogen, then those hips and boobs are just a blink of the eye away, your hair loss will be long gone and fat redistribution will finally give you the body you should have had from the start.

It's easy to get caught up in it all. I know I thought that oestrogen would solve all my body issues and change everything, and whilst it did change some things, it definitely wasn't a magic pill for all my woes. I feel sad that my boobs are still pretty tiny, even after nearly 15 years. I'm lucky in that my hair is still mostly all there, but hormones didn't make the bits that had receded grow back. I know others that have similar disappointments with their expectations of testosterone, be that it didn't make them any more muscly, or that actually even after years of hormone therapy they still struggle to grow a beard.

Our world is very visual, and very based on how we appear. It's also a binary society, and especially so when it comes to gender. It's all rubbish as well, because gender is more complex than just two things, but it sometimes still feels almost impossible not to be influenced by this binary. It's sometimes impossible not to feel sad when you don't measure up to what society tells us should make a man or a woman, even if you know it's all messed up and wrong. And, of course, if you don't fit the bill exactly, then you're more likely to be noticed by others, who could then potentially become a threat, and hello anxiety.

Anxiety and sadness for me are so linked together. I think

that for a lot of us there is this sadness within us when it comes to who we should have always been from the start. There's the loss we feel, both for what could have been, and for what doesn't happen, despite what we hope. So much of it is out of our hands as well, which makes it harder to manage.

Just to add the final icing on the cake, I also feel anxious about feeling sadness and loss, because I know that it might hurt others to know this. I feel afraid of the consequences of my sadness, which leads to anxiety, so I try and hold it together, to not show my sadness too much, which also leads to anxiety about trying to do something that I'm not that good at: holding it all together.

So, what can we do about this?

- Well, first, try and tell someone. Chances are the people around you already know something's up (from personal experience I know that I sometimes think I'm holding it together really well, when in reality I'm actually a bit of a mess when it comes to anxiety). Telling someone can really help, even though it's also really hard. It's sharing the load you're feeling and making it more manageable.

- Try and break down what you're feeling as it can help enormously long term. Like with anger, there's often a lot going on under the surface. If you can afford it, speak to a counsellor or therapist.

- Write it down. Keeping a diary can be extremely helpful, especially in terms of being able to look back at how you've been feeling lately.

- Accept it for what it is. I think this is one of the hardest things we can do, but also one of the most powerful things as well. Acceptance of the situation can be really helpful. This doesn't mean that you're giving up, but rather that you understand that some things are out of your control, so you're going to put your focus into the things that you do have control over.

I can't change the fact that I didn't have the same experiences that a cis person would have had, and I can't change the fact that I'm trans, but I can change how that makes me feel. There are things that I can do to make myself feel better, about my trans identity, about my body, and about my life.

It might not be easy, but, honestly, when was anything to do with being trans easy?

Fear

Fear and anxiety are closely linked. It's very much a part of human nature, and our bodies use fear to tell us whether something is dangerous or not.

Fear can be innate or learned. Innate fears are things that are common to us all and they're all about survival. A classic example of an innate fear is the fear of falling. It's something we're all born with and it makes sense that we have this from the start. No one wants to fall to their death, so it seems sensible to have that fear built into us.

Learned fears are things we pick up along the way. For example, when I was a kid, I found one of those huge spiders in my bed. You know the ones: big, spidery, live in beds. Anyhow, it scared me a lot, and now I'm so not down with spiders. I wasn't scared of them before this –wary maybe, but not particularly scared. I learned to be afraid of them.

Here's an interesting thing about learned fear: you don't have to have experienced that fear yourself to develop it. This makes sense from an evolutionary perspective. Say that spider was super-poisonous; it would make sense for me to tell others about it, and warn them, passing on the fear.

So, moving away from spiders for a moment (moving far, far away, obviously), let's take a look at fear, anxiety and being trans.

We know that being trans puts us at risk. The fear we experience is very real, and very anxiety-inducing. It's sometimes a very multi-layered fear as well. For example, the other day I was walking down the road and someone shouted at me. I had my headphones on, so I just carried on walking because I knew it wasn't someone I know, and normally if someone shouts at me in the street it isn't going to be anything nice. I felt a slight panic, but I also knew that if I just kept moving, it would be okay. Except the man that shouted at me didn't like that I'd decided to keep on moving. No, he decided to try and keep pace with me, walking alongside, trying to get my attention. So now that slight panic starts to turn into fear. I can hear over my headphones that he's going on about how he just wants to talk to me, and how women nowadays are all so sensitive, and why can't men talk to pretty women any more and how he's not going to attack me, or anything.

Because of course a stranger saying to you that they're not going to attack you is super-reassuring.

I wish that I could say that I told him to fuck off, or that I said a witty and empowered thing that made him back off, but I didn't, mainly because I was scared. I was scared because it was a scary situation, and I was scared because this guy was obviously trying to talk to me because he thought I was hot, but he hadn't realized I was trans.

For any woman to get harassment in the street is dangerous,

but for a trans woman there is another level of danger. We all know this because we've all been here. People behave differently when they find out we are trans, and often that behaviour becomes very unsafe for us to be around.

I'm afraid that if someone reads me as trans they might hurt me, they might even murder me. It sounds extreme, I know, but it happens. I think it's hard not to feel anxious about this. The fear of people seeing you, and seeing your identity, is a strange one, as visibility can be empowering. It's just that on a more personal level, it can also be dangerous.

Fear tends to be quite consuming, though. It's a really important survival instinct but it's also liable to make you over-react. Learned fears, especially, can be disproportional and become very consuming. Getting harassed in the street is horrible. It's loaded with potential danger, and it's right and normal to feel afraid. It's important to be aware of this possibility in order to stay safe. Like any fear, though, it can trigger a disproportionate response.

After my incident, which incidentally wasn't the first time this had happened, I didn't want to go out again. It was a struggle to even leave the house for a good month or two. And when I did go out, if I was on my own I'd make a point of avoiding any men I saw heading my way, even if it sometimes added an extra half hour, or hour even, to my journey.

Someone else I knew who experienced some street harassment only used cabs to get around for the next six months, despite it nearly bankrupting her. Another started carrying around a pair of sharp pliers in her pocket, just in case.

Fear makes us do things we wouldn't normally consider, because we want to survive. Sometimes these things are good things that actually help us to stay safe, to stay anxiety-free, but sometimes they're not. The trick, of course, is working out which is which.

Sometimes fears, fears based on real experiences especially, can become consuming and hard to break out of. You can overcome them, though. You just need to know what tools to use. Because fear and anxiety are two sides of the same coin, the ways forward are also very similar.

Telling someone about your fears can really help. However, it can be very difficult, especially if you're talking about something that happened to you, which is why it's important that you talk to someone you know you can trust.

It's worth considering talking to someone on a helpline if you don't feel like there's anyone in your life you can talk to properly. The person on the other end of the phone or web chat is there specifically to listen to what you've got to say, and it's a space where you can safely share what's going on for you. There are a lot of helplines out there. I've listed some in the back of this book if you want to know more.

It can also be helpful to remember these things:

Know that this feeling will lessen over time. Take it day by day, doing what you can, when you can.

Know that other people have felt, are feeling and will feel how you're feeling. You're not alone in this, despite how it feels.

When you get to the point of thinking about what to do about your fears and anxiety, focus on what you can change, rather than what you can't. The goal here is to feel better, and thinking about what you have no power or control over isn't going to help with that.

Find ways to soothe and calm yourself. It might be breathing exercises, meditation, distracting yourself with 90s rom-coms or going for a run. If you can find something that works for you, you can add it to your toolkit!

Feelings can be scary, and the changes these feelings create can add to our anxiety and our fears. As trans people, we are agents of change. We change ourselves and we change the people and society around us as well. This can be intense to experience, so we need to remember to allow our brains to catch up sometimes when it comes to personal change, and we need to remember, no matter how hard and unfair it may seem, to let the rest of the world catch up to us as well.

Sometimes it can feel like the rest of the world is so far behind us in terms of trans rights and understanding. This can be frustrating and cuts across all aspects of our lives, from coming out to people and them not understanding, right up to human rights issues, such as being able to access services and have protection against prejudice and discrimination.

Anxiety and the emotions that surround it can sometimes make everything feel pointless, like the world isn't changing and that everything out there is painful for us as trans people. This can make us angry or sad or scared. Honestly, it would be unusual if it didn't make us feel these things.

It's mega-important, though, to remember that things *are* changing and that, despite all this, we do have allies, we do have support and we do have love. It's often hard to see, and anxiety can really blind us to this as well, but it is out there, and that can only be a good thing to hold on to when anxiety and the emotions that come with it start to affect us.

Anxiety notes: What makes you anxious?

Feeling unsafe, being around boisterous people taking up everyone's space, unfair criticism, being underestimated and feeling unseen.

Feeling observed/being under scrutiny.

Feeling as if people around me are getting tired of me/bored of me.

Feeling that if I'd be myself (not just my transness, but my actual opinions and the things I like), it would be harder for people to like me, so I'll just try to be whatever they might like or expect from me.

Feeling that since I have no real control over an issue, and I might not immediately solve it, it may get worse and worse.

Making important phone calls, needing to leave an event and not knowing how to leave without seeming rude or distracting, presenting in front of large groups and getting tongue-tied due to my autism.

Going out, socializing in a group, fantasies about confrontation, any visit to the NHS, dancing in public.

Travel, particularly air travel, because of documents, searches, being trans, racism.

Sense of being controlled/grasped and losing myself in a relationship.

Fear that I've 'got it wrong' or might 'get it wrong', especially in public.

Going outside, walking down the street and dealing with the stares and looks from other people.

Knowing that I might never be able to get the surgery I need to feel less dysphoric, because the waiting lists are so long, and the cost of going private is so high.

The thought of coming out.

Working in a shop, constantly wondering if the next customer that comes along is going to say something transphobic or just rude.

I get very anxious every time I have to be still when I'm outside of my home: on the bus; on the tube; waiting in a queue; any time where there's opportunities for people to notice me. I've become aware that as long as I'm moving, my transness is less visible, and my anxiety reduces as well.

CHAPTER 4

Coming Out

For me, coming out is a difficult thing to talk about. It's one of those things that I'm glad I did, but it was filled with anxiety and stress at the time. It was also something I had to do numerous times, with various people. I came out to my partner, my family, to my work colleagues, to friends, then some more friends, and then new friends. In a way, coming out is an ongoing thing as well. If I change jobs, for instance, I have to think about coming out all over again, even though actually I'd probably rather not have to.

For some of us, because people see the transness in us before anything else, coming out is a constant thing. For others, it's something they have more control over, but all of it is still anxiety-inducing and difficult.

One of the more complicated comings-out for me was at my work. I worked in a shop at the time, and although the people I worked with were lovely, they were also all cis and didn't really have any understanding of trans issues. I wanted to tell them all, because they were my friends and they meant a lot to me.

Also, I wanted to do it at my own pace, because, well, that's the only way to come out.

So, anyhow, I happened to mention to another trans person – someone I'd met at a local support group – that I wasn't out at work yet. I was like 'No, I'm not out to my work yet. They're all lovely, don't get me wrong, but I just want to wait a little bit first y'know?' It was still early days for me and I was finding my feet. I'd only come out to a few close people at the time. Keeping it at my own pace, with me in control, was unsurprisingly really important to me. We carried on talking for a bit, and this person asked where I worked. Maybe you can see where this is going, right? Good on you if you can, because I sure as hell didn't.

This is where it got unpleasant and I learnt a valuable lesson: just because someone shares an identity with you, in this case being trans, it doesn't mean they're a nice person. They started on about how they believed that every trans person should be out; and if we don't come out, then we're letting other trans people down; and if we're letting other trans people down, then maybe we're not as trans as we think. They then decided that they were going to come into my place of work and out me, because I was taking too long and needed to pass this trans initiation test if I really wanted to be trans. So basically, another trans person – someone I'd known for maybe a couple of weeks at best – wanted to out me, so that I'd commit to being trans. Yeah, I've had better interactions with people.

It put me in quite a pickle because I didn't know how likely it would be that this person would come into my work, but equally I didn't want to take that risk either. In the end it worked out okay. I told my work friends, and everyone was cool, and the person that threatened to out me never made an appearance. As comings-out go, though, it wasn't the best, and it wasn't at all how I wanted to do it.

My experience is maybe an extreme version compared to many other people's, but for all of us, coming out is a big deal. It can be hugely anxiety-inducing because there's just so much to think about. There's potential anxiety about telling people, coming out to the wider world, feeling confident in how you look, and working out how you're going to do all this. Then there's all the other stuff that potentially can happen when you come out, like all the questions and the anxiety around things such as your voice, how you look (both to others and how you see yourself), hormones, and accessing the various services you personally need to help you with your transition. A lot of these are interlinked as well. I remember trying to sort out electrolysis for my facial hair and feeling so anxious about my voice on the phone when I went to book my first appointment. Now my voice isn't too bad, but for a while before I started speech therapy there was always this pause when I told people my name on the phone. Sometimes people would just go with it, but more than once I'd get some form of questioning about why I sounded like a man or why I had a girl's name.

Voice anxiety

Voice stuff is hard, as it takes work to get to where you want to be. For trans women, trying to raise our voices to an acceptable pitch (by society's standards, anyhow) takes a lot of time, speech therapy, and potentially surgery. Even then, for some people, it just never quite gets to the place they'd wish.

For trans men, testosterone can help with the lowering of the voice pitch, but it doesn't always work that way, and for some people their voices just never break. Again, speech therapy is an option (although it is often harder to find someone who will work with lowering voice pitch), but this can be expensive, time-consuming, and yet another thing to feel anxiety around.

Exercises and techniques you can practise at home to work on voice changes are especially useful if you can't access speech therapy or surgery. Thankfully, there are a lot of resources on the internet, and even some apps to help. Some are specific for the trans community, like Eva, or Christella VoiceUp (although you do have to pay for some of this in the form of in-app purchases), and others are more just for pitch analysis, like Voice Pitch Analyzer, or Praat. There are a lot of YouTube videos too, and places like Reddit – the various trans groups on there will often have lists of resources you can access, so it's always worth doing a little search in case you come across something that works for you (see Further Reading and Resources).

You can also practise at home, by doing things like singing along to musicians that you like. It's often easier to raise or lower your voice if you're trying to match someone else. You can also just listen to people's voices you like and try to emulate them. If you feel self-conscious about practising your voice in front of other people, maybe start off doing it in private, or talking to your pet in your new voice, before moving up to humans.

Remember that changing your voice is hard. It is going to take practice and perseverance. This isn't an overnight thing. Voice work is complex stuff and it can seem like yet another formidable task in a sea of overwhelming things, so here's some basic information that may help.

Generally speaking, male pitch range is anything from 60 to 180 Hz. Female pitch range is somewhere between 160 and 300 Hz. However, this is nowhere near the whole story, as pitch is just a piece of the overall puzzle. Articulation (how clearly and distinctly you speak), intonation (how your voice rises and falls – things like having a monotone voice versus a sing-song voice) and timbre (the distinctness of your voice – some people, for example, might have a husky voice, whereas others might have a silky or warm voice) are all important in how gendered your voice sounds. Where you speak from, how your tongue and throat move, your posture and how you breathe also all play a part.

It's complex stuff, and although there are guidelines when it comes to pitches, for example, there are always exceptions and variations, which can make for quite a confusing and anxiety-driven ride. Like so many things, it's about what you want to achieve and what you know is actually achievable, given your situation. This in itself is anxiety-inducing, but there are options out there when it comes to voice changes, and they are achievable options, ranging all the way from paid speech therapy to practising using videos on the internet. The trick, of course, is getting past the anxiety, taking back control and starting to do something about it.

Coming out when people don't want you to

There's a chance that when you come out to people, you might meet some opposition. Sometimes it can be families that struggle, sometimes it's friends, and sometimes it's partners if you're in a relationship. This can be really tricky. Opposition is always difficult, but when it's tied to a core part of your identity, it can quickly become unmanageable and very anxiety-inducing.

Let's take the example of what happens if you come out to your partner, for instance, and they say, 'No, I don't accept that.' What can you do if they shut down, demand that you stop doing this, or refuse to talk about it? It's almost impossible to see a way forward, especially if you also love this person. I mean, you could just carry on, as if everything is fine, never talking about it ever again, but I think we all know, deep down, that this isn't a healthy option, either for you or them. It might feel easier to do this, especially if your partner has a really strong negative reaction, but everyone hurts and everyone loses this way.

It's a hard one, because if you do make the choice to talk about being trans, then you're also making the choice to have some difficult conversations, ones that ultimately might lead to you breaking up. When I was in this exact situation, what got me through it was asking myself two extremely important questions:

'Am I happy?'

'Is my partner happy?'

It seems pretty basic, right? These questions, though, are essential life questions. If you're unhappy, then chances are your partner isn't happy either, and vice versa. And if both of you are unhappy, then both of you are going to have to do something about that.

Look at it this way. Ultimately, the only person you're going to spend your whole life with is you. This makes you pretty important. Maybe, just maybe, it might make you the most important person in your life. And, as the most important person in your life, you really need to look after you.

Sometimes doing that can be rough, and sometimes it might mean making some difficult decisions, ones that in the short term might make you feel worse. But if you're not happy, and the person you're with isn't happy, then that's not going to be sustainable.

If you've got to the point of coming out as trans to someone, even if you're unsure how they're going to react, then being trans is a part of who you are, and it's a part that you're going to have to look after and care for, especially in those early days.

You might need to make some tough decisions, and the situation might be sad for a while, but ultimately, you're being true to yourself and your partner. Whether your relationship can work through your transness, or whether it can't, ultimately you need to make sure that you're okay.

Being trans isn't always an easy journey – that much I think we can all agree on – and whenever someone you care about finds your identity difficult or chooses to reject you because of it, then you're going to feel that pain pretty badly. Whether it's your family or friends or partner/s, it almost makes no difference. It's all hard and, yeah, at times it's all shit.

The only thing you do have control over is you and your decisions. The choices you make are often going to be hard, but by centring yourself within those decisions you're also protecting yourself, and making sure that you have some semblance of control, and that in itself is as good a place to be as any when times are tough and difficult choices have to be made.

There is some further reading and resources about all this in the back of the book, so please do check that out.

Finding out who you are

We are all changing, constantly. Honestly, it can be a wild ride sometimes, and, for me, finding out who I am has been a major part of my trans history. I know, for instance, that I'm trans, and I know that I'm a woman, but what does that actually mean?

Working out where I fit within those identities has been – and if I'm being real, still is – a journey, one that really got going once I came out. Before that, so much of it was about working out if what I felt was real; and then, once I'd worked out that it was real, working out how to tell everyone about it, preferably with the minimum amount of fallout. Just doing this took so much energy and so much thought. I can't stress enough how much I thought about this, and I know that I'm not alone in this. It always makes me laugh (in a wtf sort of way) when people talk about trans people rushing into this. Rushing is the very last thing we do.

Coming out was a major part of finding out who I was, and who I am, because by coming out I'm naming something. I'm actually naming myself (both in a very real name-changing sort of way and in a metaphysical way), and by doing that I'm also allowing myself to own myself. I'm starting on that journey to find out who I am.

Like I said before, it's a wild ride, because once you start looking into who exactly you are, you also start looking into who exactly you want to be as well. There is no one way to find yourself. It's more something you work out along the way, and as trans people we often develop a very intimate and personal relationship with this journey, in part because it is so hard won, and in part because we do come at this from a unique perspective.

I know you're probably thinking that sounds like a bit of a cliché, right? But I'm not really talking about the gender thing here, or at least not the binary cis-gaze-focused man becomes woman or vice versa thing. No, I'm talking about the unique perspective of feeling that something big, something fundamental, something that everyone tells you is true about yourself, actually isn't. Not everyone feels this. Loads of people just merrily go about their business never even considering who they are, never thinking about their core. Loads of people go through their entire lives never really knowing themselves, because nothing ever makes them think about it. It just is.

We, on the other hand, we really get to think about it. Gender identity is a core part of everyone's being, but we as trans people get to make an active choice about how that looks for us. Sometimes it feels like a decision made in opposition to who we're not, but that just gives us more momentum to grow, and become the people we were always meant to be.

On Anxiety – Rory

What does anxiety look and feel like for you?
I notice when I'm exhibiting anxious behaviours. For example, I start picking at parts of my body, incessantly playing with and pulling at hairs and biting my lip or inside cheek. Sometimes I overeat when I'm not hungry at all – shovelling sugary and fatty foods down my throat. Other times, I notice that I'm kind of stuck, like I'm in a boot loop and can't get myself going. Or I can't make decisions about anything. Sometimes I can't even speak.

What do you do to feel better when you're feeling anxious?
I try to either burn it off by doing high-intensity exercise or to relax somehow, like taking a hot bath and listening to calming music. If I'm snacking, I've found that going for a walk around the block can stop the aimless eating. A change of scenery always helps, so going down to the beach or out to the countryside or into woods is really grounding. If I'm struggling to make a decision, I have to really push myself to do a simple thing that will help, like going for a short walk. Then I usually can start making a plan.

If you had one piece of advice for another trans/non-binary person who's experiencing anxiety, what would it be?
Don't beat yourself up for feeling this way. It's an understandable reaction to the world we inhabit. Be kind to yourself and find things that help.

What one thing, above all others, helps you when it comes to your anxiety?

Exercise. I cannot rate this highly enough. It's been life-changing to discover what an effect it can have on me mentally. That my body changes for the better, and my general health improves along with it is an added bonus, which helps keep everything else in check. My go-to exercise is weight-lifting as it's easy to see progress, both physically and on paper, and it can be done in short spurts.

How did you discover that exercise helped with your anxiety?

I discovered the therapeutic benefits of the gym a couple of years ago. I'd had a few really difficult months with my mental health and had seen my GP several times about it. For various reasons I was adamant not to start taking prescribed medication, so I was discussing with my doctor what options I had. I recall my GP saying he thought my issue was more anxiety than depression. Once I started framing things as anxiety, that was a game-changer for me. I knew that exercise has been proven to reduce anxiety. I realized that I could go to the gym and do something – even just one set of one exercise – and that would be an achievement. Obviously, if you're there and you succeed with that one set, it becomes easier to do another set and then maybe another exercise. Step by step rather than the whole mountain. I have a routine to follow, so I don't have to think about what I'm doing or make decisions that can feel impossible during an anxiety fog. I also know that if I'm not up to it, I can just leave and not give myself a hard time about it. I've lost count of the times I've walked into the gym and walked back out again five minutes later. After a while you begin to see results, lifting heavier weights and doing more reps. It becomes addictive, in a good way. Plus, knowing you're improving at something brings its own set of psychological rewards. And all the while, the exercise is producing endorphins, dopamine and serotonin, which make you feel good. I have a little voice in my head, my parent self, that tells me to go and work out. 'It'll be good for you,' they say. Even if I only do a little, they are proud of me for trying.

How does being trans/non-binary affect your anxiety?
It adds another layer. There's all the minority stress that goes on in the background: I know I'm different, so will I be accepted? I have past experience of discrimination and it's hard to let go of that sometimes and not fear that it will happen again. I've learnt ways of overcoming some of it. I try to be rational about what I am experiencing in the moment; what is actually happening in reality, versus what could be happening in my mind. It helps also to realize that I might not be the only person feeling this way, irrespective of identity.

CHAPTER 5

Dysphoria, Gender, Identity and Anxiety

It probably comes as no surprise that I have anxiety around my body. I'm guessing that a lot of us (both cis and trans) feel the same way. Body image is extremely complex, and our society isn't always that great at trying to promote positivity around this.

Before I transitioned, I kind of hated my body. I hated being photographed especially, as it just felt like a permanent record of who I wasn't – like something I spent all my time trying to at best ignore was suddenly made real. Of course, it all makes sense, because the body I had wasn't the body I wanted, because I was trans.

There's a common narrative that says that trans people are born into the wrong body. For some trans people this really rings true, and for a lot of other people it helps make understanding what it is to be trans (at a very basic level) easier to understand.

I think that for a while, early on, I felt like this as well. The thing is, though, after a while this narrative started to really up my anxiety levels. I started to feel trapped by my own body. It wasn't something I could ever leave. It was this cursed thing, something that just happened to me without my say. The anxiety

I was feeling was pretty horrible. It led to some quite significant depression, and feelings of helplessness. I couldn't see a way out, and for a while I just sort of gave up.

It's a strange one because objectively my body wasn't particularly masculine. I wasn't curvy but I was slender, and people would fairly regularly gender me as female. Trans bodies are complex things to navigate, especially when the only references we have are male and female bodies. I think for me this was a big part of the problem. The only frames of reference I had were the binary options. I know that within these binaries there's a lot of variation, sure, but they were all still one thing or another, and I didn't feel like either was how I was at the time.

Think about your body for a moment. Think about all the parts, the shapes, the textures. When you think about them it's hard not to gender them as well.

Soft skin? Often associated with femininity.

Muscled, toned body? Considered more masculine.

Square jawline? Again, super masculine.

Long hair? Super fem.

I know that I'm generalizing a bit here, and I don't feel at all comfortable with these things being so gendered, but sometimes what you think and feel don't matter if the world is at odds with that. It gets very complicated for us as trans people because we don't feel like the gender assigned to us is correct. If we are able, we try to do something about that, but by doing so there's also pressure to have to start trying to measure up to cis standards of what makes a particular gender identity.

As a trans woman I know that if I have long hair and wear

make-up, for example, my trans identity is more likely to be believed, because I'm conforming to what other people think a woman should be. I'm also aware that this isn't even something that just affects us as trans people either. If a cis woman cuts her hair short, people will potentially judge her. I had a friend who shaved all her hair off, and immediately people started assuming she was having a breakdown because she did something that didn't fit with the rules society had assigned to her gender.

Like I said before, it's complicated because also I want people to see me as female. That's who I am, and it makes me happy when people see me for who I am. It eases my anxiety when I'm seen as myself. It's affirming and powerful. So how do we reconcile all this? How do we feel empowered within our bodies – our amazing beautiful trans bodies – when it's so complicated?

It's important to recognize that gender roles, and gender presentation do exist. They can often be rigidly enforced by both society as a whole and by individuals, even if they're unaware they're doing it. If a boy plays with dolls, for example, then he can potentially face some stiff opposition from his family. If a girl likes to climb trees, or act in a 'rough and tumble' way, then often she will get labelled as a tomboy and told she'll grow out of it, because in the minds of the people telling her this that's not how girls should behave.

It's also important to talk about the differences between body dysmorphia and gender dysphoria. These two things are often confused and can get pretty muddled up, which really doesn't help anyone.

Let's take a look at the definitions of the two, according to the UK's National Health Service (NHS):

Body dysmorphic disorder (BDD), or body dysmorphia, is a mental health condition where a person spends a lot of time worrying about flaws in their appearance. These flaws are often unnoticeable to others.

People of any age can have BDD, but it's most common in teenagers and young adults. It can affect anyone, of any gender identity.

Having BDD does not mean you are vain or self-obsessed. It can be very upsetting and have a big impact on your life.[1]

Gender dysphoria is a term that describes a sense of unease that a person may have because of a mismatch between their biological sex and their gender identity.

This sense of unease or dissatisfaction may be so intense it can lead to depression and anxiety and have a harmful impact on daily life.

Many people with gender dysphoria have a strong, lasting desire to live a life that 'matches' or expresses their gender identity. They do this by changing the way they look and behave.

Some people with gender dysphoria, but not all, may want to use hormones and sometimes surgery to express their gender identity.

Gender dysphoria is not a mental illness, but some people may develop mental health problems because of gender dysphoria.[2]

These two things can be linked, in that people with gender dysphoria can also have BDD, but it's good to remember that BDD isn't something that just trans people have. Anyone (trans or cis) can be body dysmorphic, because it's about body image. Often,

---

1   NHS UK (2017) 'Body dysmorphic disorder (BDD).' Available at www.nhs.uk/conditions/body-dysmorphia.

2   NHS UK (2020) 'Gender dysphoria.' Available at www.nhs.uk/conditions/gender-dysphoria.

though, it's assumed that BDD is to do with being trans as well, because for some trans people body image is a significant issue. For me personally, both BDD and gender dysphoria apply, but for others, maybe thanks to a good support network, access to better mental health care or their own personal levels of dysphoria, BDD isn't so much of an issue.

It's good to know about this stuff because it can help with how you tackle your anxiety. The more you understand about what's going on for you, the more tools you'll have when it comes to managing things that come up. It's like the difference between trying to build a house with plans, or without. You'll still get a house at the end, but one is going to be a lot shakier and liable to fall down if there's a storm coming than the other.

For a long time, I felt that once I transitioned, once I started taking hormones and had surgery, my BDD would be cured. It made sense to me because I felt upset about my body because it wasn't the female body I should have had.

Doing these things should solve this problem, right?

Yeah, well, no.

I mean they definitely helped – hormones changed my body shape, surgery helped me feel more in touch with my body – but it all also made me hyperaware of which bits of me weren't right (in my eyes).

I've had some FFS. Before my initial consultation, I knew very clearly that I wanted a rhinoplasty. I felt that my nose was very masculine, way too pointy and large, and not at all the cute nose I wanted. I thought that was all that was needed to help me with my end goal of looking more femme, to help me like my face again.

The consultation went extremely well. The surgeon agreed with me about my nose, but he suggested that I get my forehead and hairline done as well. These were two things I was aware of, sure, but hadn't really considered because I thought they were okay. Now, because someone pointed them out, I started to feel that maybe these two things were not actually okay at all. I know that the surgeon pointed this out to help make sure I had all the information I needed, but it also made me start thinking about other aspects of my body I might have previously missed. I hadn't previously thought my hairline was that bad and no one had commented on it before, but now I felt concerned: Is it something that might make people assume I'm not female? Should I consider getting this done as well?

In the end, I decided to have my forehead done because, objectively, the surgeon was right. My forehead was another pointer towards people reading me as male, and my end goal was for people to read me as female, or at least as how society perceives being female.

Sometimes, when my gender dysphoria is bad, all I can see is how masculine I still am. I become hyperaware of things like my previously unnoticed hairline, my slight Adam's apple, my height, my large hands. I feel like what I see is a poor facsimile of what I've been told a woman should be.

When my body dysmorphia is bad, I still see all these things, but it also feels so confusing. I see the bits that are femme, and the bits that are masc, and I don't know what I'm looking at. All I do know is that to me it's ugly. It can feel like reconciling these things is beyond my ability because the feelings are strong. The anxiety can become overwhelming and stop me from even beginning to be able to think clearly for a second about what's really going on. I stop being able to see my trans body as what it is: a trans body. I see it in such gendered ways that it becomes all-consuming and I lose sight of what is actually happening.

It's incredibly difficult to not have anxiety around our bodies. We live in a world where trans people are stigmatized, attacked and ridiculed. Certain sections of society actively go out of their way to hurt us. Sometimes it's just assholes on the internet, but sometimes it's our governments, our families, or people we thought would help us in our battle for recognition and human rights.

Our bodies are gendered by other people, often before we've even left the womb, and then recorded on bits of official paper. For most people, this works just fine, but for trans people, whose bodies are at odds with their identity, it can be a real nightmare. It's no wonder we feel anxiety and stress around our bodies, and it makes it increasingly hard to love who we are.

So how do we get over this? How can we reduce the anxiety around our bodies, around our dysphoria and dysmorphia?

Techniques to try

As with everything else, there isn't a quick fix. These things take time and perseverance, and again, they won't cure your anxiety as such, because you can't get rid of anxiety completely; however, they will make it easier when the anxiety hits.

Exposure therapy

Exposure therapy is a well-known technique used in behaviour therapy. It's often used in relation to phobias, so if you were afraid of spiders, for instance, then you'd gradually get exposed to different spiders until you became used to them. Although it's not quite the same, as we're not afraid of our bodies as such, the basic principle can work well for body stuff.

Something that helped me immensely, for example, was self-portrait photography. For a couple of years, I took a photo of myself every day. I'd try to be as creative as my head would allow me, and I tried to focus first on individual parts of my body, slowly working my way up towards the bits that I found more challenging. My thinking behind this was to try and find beauty in what I am, by recording it. I mentioned before that as a teenager I hated having my photo taken, so for me this was also very empowering, as I was making the choices about how I wanted to be seen, and how I wanted to look. As time went on, this project became a way for me to reclaim my body and take ownership again, and as a plus I ended up with some lovely pictures of myself.

Starting small

There's a pressure to go all-in when it comes to solving things that upset us. Go big or go home; if you don't do it all now, then you might as well not bother. The usual inner voice stuff. With anxiety around our bodies, this isn't very helpful. Our bodies are complex and different, and that can be tricky to take on all in one go.

Find a part of you that you don't mind, ideally a part of you that you like. It can be as big or small as you want. For me it's the freckles on my face. I love those little speckles, despite not always loving the face that they sit on. Think about why you love them. I love my freckles because they're unusual. They look really beautiful and I love how much they change when I get a bit of sun on me. I love how they get stronger and brighter, and how I have them all over my body. It's like having this really cool marking on me, a tattoo I was born with.

Write down what you feel about this thing you like. Take a picture of it, journal it, record it for later.

Do this every day or week or month with a different bit of yourself. Keep writing it down, and nurturing the feelings you have towards the bits of you that work.

Use this love, or 'like' if 'love' is too strong a word right now, to help you find the beauty in the bits you aren't so keen on.

If you feel very brave, and have someone you trust, ask them to do this same exercise with their body, and compare notes. It might surprise you.

Start small and let it grow from there.

Surgeries

It feels like quite a jump to go from learning to love yourself to surgery, but bear with me. Learning to love your body is an amazing starting point, and it's even more amazing if this is enough for you and where you are in your journey.

Sometimes, though, there's only so far you can go. I think that in relation to surgeries it's worth mentioning that it can be very hardcore, but it can also be very effective when you feel like there's no other place you can go.

I think developing the tools you need to love the parts of you that you can is very important, as it gives you the bedrock you'll need when it comes to surgeries. I know that, as someone who has both learnt to love my body and had various surgeries, it made such a difference to my outlook.

Exploring my body, and discovering what I loved and what I didn't, gave me focus. It showed me what I could change and what I couldn't. Knowing this enabled me to do more precise and effective research on what was available to me when it came to surgeries.

I've had forehead reconstruction, a rhinoplasty, a tracheal shave and a cricothyroid approximation (voice pitch surgery). These were things I felt I really needed to change about myself, and they were things that I couldn't go any further with in terms of body positivity.

The surgeries were rough, and although I'm glad I did them, I wouldn't want to do them again. It's not an easy way out by any means, despite how 'cosmetic' surgery is sometimes portrayed.

It is, however, a solution that can work. I just wasn't able to love my nose, for example. I had some surgery, and now I do. I look at surgery as correcting the things that went wrong for me because of my testosterone-based puberty.

If you are thinking about surgery, there are some things to consider.

- It's not cheap. You're going to need money, both for the cost of the actual surgery and for the recovery period, which can be quite a while, depending on what you have done.

- It's not easy. It's painful, and recovery is often challenging, depending on the surgery and how quickly you heal. It can also take a toll mentally at first, and it's not unusual to feel regret and doubt at what you've done.

- You can get a lot done nowadays, but it's worth thinking about what really matters to you, and what you can and can't cope with, both in terms of your body and your wellbeing. Research is your friend here!

- Try and get as many first-hand experiences from other people as you can. The internet is a goldmine for this sort of stuff. Reddit in particular has a lot of information and other people's experiences of surgery, both from a trans and cis point of view (see Further Reading and Resources). The more you know, the better you'll be prepared.

- Surgery in itself is anxiety-inducing. It may seem kind of obvious, but it's worth pointing out just the same. The waiting before your surgery date, the cost, the actual surgery and the recovery can all feel very full-on and extreme at times. This isn't necessarily a warning sign that you shouldn't go ahead; it's more just that having any sort of surgery is very scary. It makes sense that it would create anxiety because it comes with real risks, including death. I mean, you most likely won't die, but it's definitely not a light undertaking, so it's standard to feel some anxiety at some point.

Not trans enough

We live in quite a judgey world. There's a lot of comparing our-selves to each other, a lot of competition, and a lot of judgement about who we are and if we're valid enough to be who we say we are.

This judgement is everywhere: in the media, in advertising, from ourselves and from each other, and it's something that affects us all, trans and cis. Everyone is judged on their identity and their lives, be that how manly or femme you are, how suc-cessful you are, or any other number of things.

We all know this, and of course like so many things, as trans people we're already on the back foot, so to speak. We're still very much othered by a lot of society, and often seen as lesser in comparison to cis people.

For example, when I first came out, I was met with a whole range of reactions, with a lot of them being pretty negative, judgement-based or invalidating.

Here are just a few classics I heard in relation to my identity as a trans woman:

'Why can't you just be a gay man?'

'Once you start dating again, you'll go back to who you really are.'

'You can't be a woman, because you played with cars as a child.'

'I don't believe you.'

'I don't think being transgender is real, so I'm going to keep using your proper name.'

'I don't like your new name, so I'm not going to use it.'

'But you're too tall to be a woman.'

'I think you need to see someone because this isn't normal.'

'Are you having a breakdown?'

Clearly all these comments are not great for anyone's wellbeing. They're anxiety-inducing, dismissive, and invalidating of identity, which can make you feel like you're not being heard at all.

You're basically being told that you're not who you think you are, and whilst it's good to explore who you are, these sorts of comments are not the place to start from when you're doing that.

Invalidation of trans identities is everywhere, even within our own communities. I've heard people say that unless you have gender reassignment surgery, then you're not really trans, or that if you don't have intense dysphoria all the time then you're not valid.

It's not great.

In today's world it's extra tough as well because we're all so on show all the time. Visibility is great but it also has negative consequences. Unrealistic expectations and stereotypes are often forced upon people, leading to more anxiety and feelings of not living up to normative gender roles, especially if, actually, that's not something you even want to do.

It's easy to not feel enough of anything to count, be that being male, female or trans. Society has strong ideals of what all these things should look like, and if you don't fit, if you can't or don't want to live up to the expectations of what a man/ woman should be in a cis-normative world, then things start to look somewhat rough.

So, what can we do? How do you tackle anxiety that's rooted around who you are, especially if it's constantly invalidated and dismissed by the world around you? Well, for starters, remember you are valid and you are real. Stay grounded in this as your starting point.

- Repeat in your head, 'I know myself and I know how I feel.' If you can and if it's safe to do so, say it out loud, shout it from the rooftops, validate yourself.

- Don't let other people grind you down. I know, easier said than done, but do your best not to let it get to you.

- If you can, cut out the toxic people in your life. If you can't right now, then make plans for when you can.

- Challenge when you're able to. It's incredibly important to always stay safe, and not put yourself in harm's way if you can avoid it, but sometimes it can be really empowering to assert yourself and say, 'I'm sorry but you're wrong about that.' (Note that this is different to arguing about your identity with someone. When someone refuses to listen to what you're saying, then it might be best to remove yourself from the situation, if at all possible.)

- Understand that some people won't change their minds. This is a tough life lesson, but you can't change everybody.

· Use your anxiety to warn you if things feel unsafe, but don't let it take over completely. At its core, anxiety is your body telling you something isn't right. Often this warning system reacts disproportionally to threats, but it's also very important to listen in specific situations where things might escalate and you might find yourself in an unsafe position.

Identity can be fluid. This is often seen as a bad thing, and people tend to latch onto this to dismiss others' identities, but both gender and sexual fluidity are real. It's normal, and part of who we are as humans. As we grow, and exist in this world, our thoughts and ideas change, so it makes sense that sometimes our identities can be fluid as well. Some people know very clearly that they are trans or non-binary, whereas for others it might take a while to get there. Some might realize that they're not trans after all, and some might reach a place where the gender binaries of male and female just don't work with how they feel inside.

The journey is often as important as the destination, and even when you get to where you think you're going, it might just give you a better viewpoint to get to somewhere new. The important thing is to know that how you are feeling is valid. If you think you're trans, then it's something you should definitely explore further, because who knows? You might well be. And if after exploring you discover that actually you're not trans after all, then think of this as part of your journey to discover yourself. Finding out who you're not is as important as finding out who you are. Anxiety about your identity is a really common thing, and you're 100 per cent not alone in this. It's very normal, and very real.

Other people questioning your identity is, sadly, also a very common thing, and it can be extremely anxiety-inducing and difficult to deal with. It's important to remember that a lot of the time when people say things like 'I don't believe you're trans' or 'You're wrong about this and I'll never accept it,' actually they're saying more about themselves than about you. Although it's still hurtful and unkind to hear these things, especially when it's from people who mean something to you, it can be helpful to remember that point. For example, when someone says that they don't believe you, or that they don't understand why you'd say something like this, what they're actually saying is 'This is very new to me and I can't deal with it right now.' Again, it's not an easy thing to hear, but sometimes people do need time.

When people invalidate your trans identity by saying you're not trans unless you have surgery, for instance, or that you can only be trans if you identify as a binary gender, then what they're actually saying is 'This is something that doesn't match up with my experience, and I thought my experience was the only way people transitioned. This is new to me.'

People often struggle with new things, especially if they're new things that relate personally to them. They can take it as a personal attack on them and how they are. They can feel threatened or attacked, even if this isn't your intention.

Parents and caregivers can sometimes struggle with their children coming out as trans, in part because they can feel that they've done something wrong. Being trans is often portrayed as a negative thing within our world, especially via the media, so they may associate transness with childhood trauma and see it as a bad thing to happen to anyone, let alone their child. They may also be worried about the hardships you're going to potentially face as a trans person, and they express this by trying to deny your transness. To us this may not make much sense, but when emotions are involved, sense often goes out the window.

What we feel can be a powerful thing. We know this as trans people because it's what drives us to explore who we are.

Often when we feel anxiety about our identity that's brought on by others, knowing why people react the way they do can help, as it gives context. It doesn't always make it easier in terms of the hurt and pain it causes, but it can help with lessening anxiety if we know that actually it's not our fault.

So, let's recap a little, with some key things to remember:

- Know that you are valid, and your identity is real.

- Explore who you are, using the tools available to you. This could be as simple as talking to other people like yourself, right up to therapy and beyond.

- Stay safe and, if you can, try and remove yourself from situations that feel unsafe.

- Don't feel you need to fight every battle.

- Take time for yourself where you don't have to think about your trans identity. If this is difficult, distract yourself with films, going for a run or a hobby.

- You are valid, and your trans identity is real.

On Anxiety – Roch

What does anxiety look and feel like to you?

My experience of anxiety varies – there have been times when I have felt unable to breathe but couldn't figure out why. Other times, I have had palpitations and felt an overwhelming sense of dread. My standard, low-level experience of anxiety sits in the pit of my stomach, and in a tightening in my neck and shoulder.

What do you do to feel better when you're feeling anxious?
I have recently started mindfulness practice and have been doing yoga for the past year or so. Yoga has been really helpful for relaxing the physical tension I'm feeling. I find that, when my anxiety is originating from negative self-talk or overthinking, I watch Bob Ross,[3] just to hear some positive talk and affirmations. Going for a walk or engaging in movement helps me feel less trapped.

If you had one piece of advice for another trans/non-binary person who's experiencing anxiety, what would it be?
Focusing on a slow, deep breath out – this helps engage the parasympathetic nervous system, which counteracts the part of our physiological reactions that make us feel so awful – it can help slow heart rate and reduce the sensation of palpitations. This can help make things feel less intense, and also reminds us to breathe.

What one thing, above all others, helps you when it comes to your anxiety?
For me, it's not one thing over others – it's a combination of factors and interventions that work together to reduce the feelings of anxiety or acknowledge the situation I'm facing. I suppose I would say that focusing on the things I do have control over, or things that I can change, is helpful.

How does being trans/non-binary affect your anxiety?
Anxiety is a rational response. It's our brain trying to keep us safe by alerting us to a potential threat and preparing our body to respond to the perceived threat. As trans people, there are

---

3   Bob Ross (1942–1995) was an American painter, who was widely known for his television series, *The Joy of Painting*.

naturally more threats that we have to respond to, which means we can become hypervigilant to threats, and so our bodies continue to display unpleasant and distressing physiological responses.

So, our sphere of experience can become occupied with monitoring for, and responding to, threat. And I think it's important to recognize that, while we can talk about individual ways that we can respond to such anxiety and manage those feelings (because we can never eliminate threats from our existence), trans people and other marginalized identities are more often than not exposed to threats that result from systemic oppression and violence, and that is not okay. Monitoring for a sabre-tooth tiger or a car coming along the road should be expected. Having to worry about how a health care professional treats us, or how someone on the street responds to us because of our identity, should not be part of our experiences and life. And this is where a lot of focus needs to be placed with regard to challenging and dismantling the systems and structures that contribute to our oppression and disenfranchisement.

CHAPTER 6

Social Anxiety

Social anxiety is, at its simplest, a fear of social situations. It's normally pretty intense and can make you start to dread social events and talking to people. It can stem from a fear of being judged or rejected by others in a social setting, and often leads to low self-esteem. It can make life incredibly difficult for a lot of people, making interactions virtually impossible, which in turn can make isolation become a real problem.

Basically, it's pretty shit.

Anyone can experience moments of social anxiety, and it's perhaps one of the most common forms of anxiety. Feeling worried or nervous about talking in front of some other people, or struggling to make eye contact with others? That's social anxiety.

When these feelings start to get overwhelming and impact your everyday life, then social anxiety (or social phobia as it's also known) can become something we call social anxiety disorder. There are quite a lot of different symptoms of social anxiety disorder, but here are some of the more common ones, to give you an idea:

- fear of situations where you feel you might face judgement

- feeling anxious about upcoming social events

- strong and intense fear of talking with people you don't know, especially in a new, or unknown social setting, like a wedding for example

- being hyperaware of any physical symptoms of your anxiety, like blushing or shaking, and what people will think when they notice them

- avoiding doing things or speaking to people out of fear of embarrassment

- trying your best to never be the centre of attention

- worries that you'll embarrass yourself or say something inappropriate or stupid

- trying to hide your anxiety and feeling like you're doing a terrible job of it, making you more anxious

- being super self-critical when it comes to your place within your social circles, and over-analysing every interaction you have with other people, just in case you did something wrong.

Social anxiety also has physical symptoms, including things like:

- blushing

- forgetfulness

- tense feelings in your muscles, and cramp

- feeling dizzy, or a bit woozy

- breathing problems, such as struggling to catch your breath

- shaking or trembling

- stomach aches, or nausea

- increased heart rate

- sweating.

If you experience social anxiety, it can sometimes come across as being reclusive, unfriendly or rude, even when that's not the case. That's because people often struggle to recognize social anxiety in others. I know my own social anxiety has meant that I've been labelled as one of those difficult, standoffish people, which again just heightens any social anxiety I already feel.

As a trans person, social anxiety is particularly problematic because it often feels like we're already at a disadvantage. We are already 'othered' by people, just by being trans. It's nearly always the first thing people notice about us, and it very much affects how people interact with us as well. For instance, once people know my trans status, it's more likely that they'll misgender me, accidentally or otherwise, even if previously they'd been happily using the right pronouns. Many trans people I've told this to have had this happen to them as well, even if they 'pass' in cis society as their gender.

When people see us and our trans identities, they often also start to scrutinize us – staring, asking ridiculous questions, and even shouting at and mocking us. This makes it hard to be able to interact with other people because it creates social anxiety, with the depressing caveat that in a lot of trans people's cases it's actually justified and a real anxiety, based on a real threat. Sadly, I don't know a single trans person who hasn't experienced some form of abuse from other people, be that verbal, physical or emotional.

It gets really bleak, because trans people are often painted as this threat to society by hate groups, and even worse, by hate groups made up of people that you'd normally think would be the last people to do this. You only have to take a brief look at certain websites and social media platforms to see feminist extremists, and alliances of other people within our LGBTQ+ community banding up to preach about how dangerous trans people are, and how our gender ideology (basically us wanting to exist and live without fear of our human rights being taken away) is destroying society. It's almost funny that the people preaching all this hate are the ones that are saying we're a threat. It's no wonder we're all so anxious.

It's rough, and it can feel unmanageable. For me personally, social anxiety is one of the hardest things to overcome, in part because we have to interact with other people in order to function in the world we live in today. It's like we don't really have a choice in it, which isn't ideal when social anxiety is such a big thing in our lives.

Things that can help with social anxiety

I'm not going to lie, it's a long road when it comes to social anxiety. Here are some of the things that have helped me:

Keeping a diary
I find it's helpful to write about how I feel. It gets things out of my head and helps me process what's going on. It can also be really useful to look back at how you felt in the past, if only to

know that you got through those feelings, and that you are more resilient than you sometimes give yourself credit for.

Work out what you're comfortable with at any given time
Social anxiety can ebb and flow. Sometimes it can be very full-on and sometimes it eases off, so try to go with that. If you're out with friends and it starts getting a bit much, then you can leave. If you're in a cafe and it starts to get too busy for you, then head off. If you're having a very anxious day, you don't always have to go out. Listening to what your mind and body are saying is extremely important. Sometimes it's good to push those limits, but also sometimes it's good to listen to them, and respect what they're telling you.

Breathing
Slow breathing can help enormously with social anxiety. It lowers your heart rate, which in turn can help reduce panic symptoms and the anxiety that comes with them. Many, many times I've excused myself to go to the toilet, just so I can compose myself and get that social anxiety back under control with some breathing exercises!

Be truthful with your friends
This isn't always easy, but it can help to tell the people you're close to that you have social anxiety. If they know more about what's going on for you, it might feel easier to tell them that you're not in the mood for meeting up because you're feeling anxious.

Sharing can also help in terms of support as you'll feel more able to say if you need a minute, for instance, when you're out and about with these people. Also, you might be surprised by who else then feels okay to share about their social anxieties as well!

Find other trans/queer people that get you

A lot of my social anxiety is based on others judging my trans-ness. Finding other trans people like me helped enormously, as suddenly I didn't have to worry about that.

It's worth pointing out that just because someone is trans it doesn't mean you're going to be best friends. We are all different, but if you can find people that genuinely 'get' and like you, it can help a lot with social anxiety. Finding people is hard – like I said, it's a long road – and sometimes that can mean pushing yourself a little by going to trans support groups or engaging in internet forums, but in the long term it can really pay off.

Medication

Another option for social anxiety is medication. There are various things that can be prescribed for anxiety disorders by your GP, including beta blockers, benzodiazepines and antidepressants. There are also various herbal treatments you can try, but, as always, check with your doctor first!

Social media

Let's talk social media for a second. For me, social media is very linked into my anxiety, and I suspect that I'm not the only one.

I have times where I very deliberately delete Twitter, Face-book and Instagram from my phone. In the case of Facebook, I actually deleted my profile permanently, because it just became too much for me. I think that with social media it's easy to get fatigued by it all. I found that it started to overwhelm and consume me, because it's just so constant and full-on. Everything you say is up for scrutiny by everyone else, whether you know them or not, and everyone has an opinion.

Everyone loves to chip in on our stuff especially – trans issues are ripe for the picking – and it often feels like everyone has something to contribute. (Obviously, by 'contribute' I mean they tell us that we're wrong about who we are, that there are only two genders, that trans people don't exist, and that we should all be put in a camp somewhere so we don't pollute 'normal' people.)

The trouble with social media is that it polarizes everything. It works us all up and then steps back, rubbing its little hands with glee, to watch the chaos. It can get incredibly toxic and, obviously, toxicity can be very damaging for anxiety.

Getting rid of Facebook was one of the most positive things I've done for myself in a long while. The thing is, that was just me. I could tell all of you to get rid of Facebook – it didn't work for me, right, so it must be awful for everyone else too. Except that this is exactly what I've been talking about: polarization. When transphobes tell us that we don't exist, what they actually mean is they're not trans, so it can't be a thing. If they don't have it, then it can't be real, because it's not part of their world. And, yes, I know it's slightly more nuanced than that. Just because someone's never had measles, it doesn't mean they'll not believe in it (although honestly, I wouldn't hold my breath on that being true for everyone). Just because something works for you, it doesn't mean that it's right for everyone else.

Limiting social media for me was extremely helpful for my anxiety, but for others social media might well be the only place they get to talk to other trans people. It might be vital to their wellbeing and they might see it as a really positive thing.

I once told a friend about how much I hated social media, about how toxic and dangerous it was. I was on a real rant about it, like screw it all, burn it to the ground, the world would be better off without it. For her, though, this just wasn't the case. She was surprised about how much I hated it. I know what you're thinking, she was cis, yeah? She didn't experience the hate and toxicity we as trans people do, yeah? Well, no. She was very aware of the crap against us out there. She was trans herself. She just found social media more helpful than detrimental. She had online friends that became real-life friends. She had a community of people out there supporting her, who she was then able to support as well. She filtered the hate out, she didn't engage with any trolls, she used social media to be, well, social.

We are all different, and we all engage with things differently. What works for one of us might not work for another. The trick, as always, is working out what works for us as individuals, and then sharing that with no expectation that it'll work for others. With that in mind, here are some things that helped me and that may also help you.

If social media is getting too much, then get rid of it

You don't have to do it forever. Most platforms let you suspend an account rather than delete it, but take a break if it's all a bit overwhelming. Like so much else in life, if it hurts you, stop doing it.

Choose how you communicate

Communicate in ways that feel appropriate to the situation. There are loads of options for talking to people via social media, and it's good to think about the ways you're doing this. Obviously, we all know to be careful on the internet as some people out there are predators looking for targets, but equally some are just like us.

Don't feed the trolls

Here's the honest truth on this. You're unlikely to change their minds. Don't engage, because that's what they want and it's not worth it. You're the one that'll get hurt. They'll just be typing away, winding you up for the lols, hoping you'll say something they can then use against you. A lot of the time people say 'controversial' things on the internet just to see what happens. Some people mean what they say, but also some are just trying to sow chaos. Ultimately, there are better ways to change hearts and minds than fighting with random people on the internet.

Think about what you're putting out there

I'm not saying censor yourself but I am saying that once something is out there on the internet, then it's out there for ever. Think about the audience you're sharing it with. Is it just friends or is it everyone?

Like, suppose you've taken a selfie and you really like it (I know, sounds far-fetched, right, but trust me, it happens). Putting it out there is cool and all, but do you want to put it out there for your mates to see how gorgeous you are or do you want to put it out there for the world to see how gorgeous you are? Both are valid choices, but one has definitely more risk attached to it in terms of negative consequences and potential anxiety.

It's okay to have private things

It's easy to feel you need to share everything about yourself, and that you're not keeping it real if you don't, but you don't have to do this. There's a lot of anxiety attached to sharing. It's easy to get caught up in it. We have whole social media campaigns about it, which can be very powerful; but, equally, don't feel pressure to share stuff you don't feel comfortable sharing. Once it's out there, you can't really take it back.

Make social media work for you

Use it to make connections with others, use it to create community, use it to learn, and use it to change the world for the better.

Social media is an incredibly powerful tool. It's why all the people in power use it. It can be easily corrupted and used against us, and it's very addictive and engaging. It draws you in, practically daring you to respond to everything on it, even if this isn't always the wisest thing to do.

Think of it as like crossing the road. You could just rush out into the oncoming traffic because those cars, right? Those cars with their polluting and their noise, they make me so ANGRY. I'm just gonna get stuck in there and show them what for. And then get really hurt when the cars run me over because they're cars and I'm a fleshy human.

Alternatively, you could stop. You could see those noisy, dirty cars messing up the environment, and think to yourself that you're not down with this at all, but also right now if you do anything you're just going to get hurt. And the more hurt you get, the less you'll be able to do later. So instead, you go home and start a campaign about the pollution in your city, or you tell your friends and then organize a protest.

Rushing in is fine but ultimately it isn't always best when you're outnumbered. Cars, or internet haters, are going to just carry on doing their thing, even if it sucks. What matters is what you do and how that affects you.

Anxiety notes: What do you do to make anxiety better?

I get behind a locked door alone (bathroom cubicles!). I immerse myself in interests – gaming, VR, box sets, etc. I tell trusted friends on Messenger as I can't talk. I take diazepam before it builds to a meltdown. I use my home as a sanctuary.

Breathing. Closing into myself. If I can, I try to put some space between the situation that is making me feel anxious and me.

Sometimes I can't know what is making me feel anxious and I'll spend half the day feeling like my stomach is twisted, without knowing why. I don't have anxiety attacks, I just feel like I have a hum – soft, but constant – that makes me feel uneasy. Usually what turns off my anxiety is comparing it to other things that are huge and then I don't care about what's bothering me – for example, the universe, the sea, how time passes so 'this too shall pass'. The thing that works for me is showing myself it's okay to worry about something, but that it might not deserve the time I spend steeping in it.

I listen to music that calms me and play games that I enjoy. I also talk to people in my close circle if I feel I can do so.

I set easily achievable goals, encourage myself lots, try to breathe, balance taking risks with sometimes avoiding them.

I spoon my dog and eat loads of crap.

I try to remind myself that it's okay – in fact, inevitable – to make mistakes and fail at things. It doesn't make you a bad person, and if you take responsibility for it and are open about it, that can be a big relief – rather than hiding it and trying to cover it up.

I write down what I'm feeling and why, and I evaluate it. I'm open about having anxiety within my friendship group. I use medication without feeling ashamed. I listen to music that gets me moving and breaks the thought spiral and frozen sensation (the *Frozen II* soundtrack is already an instant anti-anxiety classic!).

Having others remind me that they too have those anxieties makes me feel more understandable. I try to find more perspective and remember how small I am in the world, and how everybody else has all their stuff going on. When I manage to stay with the feeling, I find kindness for myself and others through it, instead of trying to avoid it or fight it.

I try to remind myself that anxiety goes hand in hand with courage. It's only when we're frightened that we can be brave – and being trans/non-binary is an act of incredible bravery in a binary cis-normative world.

CHAPTER 7

Getting What You Need from Life

Transitioning can be an anxiety-inducing experience. I say *it can be* because we're all different and we all have different resources and experiences at our disposal. Some of us might have more money or better support systems in place than others, and these things can definitely make everything much easier. I think, though, despite where you're coming from in your transition, it's safe to say we all will get anxiety about it somewhere along the line.

As an example, here are the things that gave me varying degrees of anxiety during my transition (and sometimes still do):

- money
- surgeries
- doctors
- family
- relationships
- dating

- work
- gatekeeping
- hormones
- other people
- myself
- my trans identity
- coming out
- toilets
- pretty much everything in life.

I could go on, but I think you get the picture.

Some of these things gave me more anxiety than others. Things like money, surgery, coming out and dating particularly caused me a lot of grief, so I'm going to go into more detail about some of these things below.

Public toilets, changing rooms and single-sex spaces/services

These things scare me sometimes. I say 'sometimes', but I mean most times really. For trans people, all these spaces can be problematic and anxiety-inducing because of how some non-trans people perceive us. I've had bad experiences in all these spaces, and certainly from this, and hearing about other trans people's experiences, I know that I'm not alone.

Here in the UK, in theory according to the law right now in 2020, trans people should be able to use the toilet they want to use, access the correct changing rooms, and be eligible for services they need that are appropriate to their gender identity. In other countries this differs significantly. Currently in the USA there's an ongoing battle around various discriminatory bathroom bills that are being pushed through, which prevent trans people from using the correct toilets and gender-segregated facilities.

The thing is, though, actually it doesn't always matter what the law says, because if you walk into a toilet and someone starts shouting at you, then it's going to feel kind of irrelevant at that moment. It's a horrible reality for a lot of us, and the anxiety around this can be through the roof. It can limit so much of what you can safely do and make you have to adapt in ways you just shouldn't have to.

If you want to join a gym, say, then you also have to think about how the changing rooms are going to work. Are they going to be okay with me using them? Am I going to be okay if I choose to use them? Do I ask someone and then potentially out myself? Or is it easier to just get changed at home before I go?

Taking it a step further, what happens if you need to access rape crisis services, or sexual health information, or shelters for things like homelessness or domestic violence? These spaces are often gendered, and depending on where you are with your transition, or how you're perceived by others, these very necessary spaces might feel impossible to access.

The worst thing about all this is that there are no easy answers or solutions. Or at least no solutions that actually help to normalize our lives.

Options for easing anxiety around public toilets are finding ones where you live that are non-gendered or unisex, which is fine if you know where they are, but not so great if you're somewhere new or there just aren't any.

Inevitably, if you want to find out how trans-friendly your gym or health centre is, then you're probably going to have to out yourself by asking, 'Is this place safe for me as a trans person?'

Accessing gendered crisis services also means potentially outing yourself if it's not clear that they're trans inclusive, and even then it can be hit and miss as to what their definition of trans inclusiveness is.

It's all not ideal, and can feel very depressing, anxiety-inducing and negative.

However, there are some things you can do to help with this. Like I said before, there are no easy solutions to a lot of this – our world isn't particularly set up for us as trans people – but there are options for making it a tiny bit better, at least until our world does become better at this sort of stuff.

Ask a friend to come along

Doing things with someone you trust can make a huge difference. When there's two of you, you've got back-up, moral support, and someone to kick ass if you need it. Support from others is really important and can help make challenging things much more manageable. If you're with someone else, other people are way less likely to give you trouble, especially if that person is someone perceived to fit in the space you're in.

For example, as a trans woman I feel a lot safer using a public toilet if I'm with a cis woman. It's as if their cisness validates why I'm there, and I become cis-shaped by association.

This isn't ideal and makes me sort of hate the world, but it does mean I can pee in peace when I'm out and about, so swings and roundabouts I guess?

Find out what spaces are trans inclusive

There are some places with proven track records of being trans inclusive. Sometimes this is because there are trans people involved with that space, and sometimes it's just because loads of us use that space. These spaces are out there, you just have to find them.

The internet is a wonderful resource for finding this information, and you can also ask other trans people about their experiences. If there are any local LGBTQ+ charities or organizations in your area, they may well have a good idea of where it is safe for you to go as well. Some may even have a list of recommended trans-safe spaces and organizations.

Money and work

As trans people, we are more likely to be unemployed or unable to work. We are more likely to face discrimination and prejudice when seeking employment. And if we are lucky enough to be employed, we're still at a higher risk of facing discrimination and transphobia within the workplace.

We're more likely to be underemployed and have a lower income than our non-transgender colleagues. There are various research papers backing this up, including 'A broken bargain for transgender workers'[1] and the 'Stonewall trans report',[2] for example.

There's also a lot of personal experience evidence. The last time I was unemployed, for instance, it took me a long time to

1   Movement Advancement Project, National Center for Transgender Equality, Human Rights Campaign, and Center for American Progress (2013) 'A Broken Bargain for Transgender Workers.' Available at www.lgbtmap.org/transgender-workers.

2   Bachmann, C.L. (Stonewall) and Gooch, B. (YouGov) (2018) 'LGBT in Britain: Trans Report.' Available at www.stonewall.org.uk/system/files/lgbt_in_britain_-_trans_report_final.pdf.

find a job. I attended interviews where, as soon as they saw me, I could tell from their faces that this job wasn't going to happen. I had one interview that lasted ten minutes, where every time I tried to answer the question, they cut me off to move to the next one.

And when I have managed to get a job, I've heard some real gems when it comes to inappropriateness and ignorance. One boss told me that he only employed me because I was pretty and 'didn't look like a trans'. Another told me that he was thinking about employing more people like me (trans women) because he didn't have to worry about us getting pregnant.

It's stressful as hell. We are more likely to experience mental and physical health issues because of all this, and it can quickly become a vicious circle where everything becomes a battle.

So, what can we do to make this better? Below are some of the things that helped me, which might also be useful for you!

Stay positive

If you're looking for work and it feels like you're not getting anywhere, remember that this is just now. The future is still out there and yours for the taking.

It's easy to get disheartened by all the rejection, but use this rejection as a tool. These places were not for you, but the place that is will be out there. I know this might feel a little hollow when you're in the thick of it all, but it can be really helpful to remind yourself that there is still hope.

Research

Try and find out if there are places where you live that are trans-friendly workplaces. Stonewall has a list of top trans-inclusive employers (see the Resources section), and depending on what sort of work you're looking for, it might be worth taking a look around or asking others about their experiences. Again, connecting with local LGBTQ+ charities, helplines and trans groups might also be helpful in getting the lowdown on trans-friendly workplaces.

Plan

Work out what you want to do:

Are you looking for a career job, or something that will pay the bills?

Do you want to start something up yourself, but need a financial cushion for everyday living?

Are you going to try and start saving for anything?

Work out all these things so that you have a plan. It'll make everything else that much easier if you have an idea of what you want and your expectations around this.

If you have a job and it's causing you anxiety, it can also help to start making a plan. Work out what your triggers are and what you can do to mitigate them. If, for instance, you feel stressed and anxious about answering the phone all the time, then find out if there's a way you can do less of that. If you get anxious every time the office gets busy, then make some time when it calms down to go for a walk. Knowing that there's an end can really help.

You can also find out if your workplace can make reasonable adjustments for your anxiety. Some places offer mental health days or allow for more flexible working. Depending on where you live, you may also have legal rights in your workplace, both around mental health and gender identity. In the UK, we have the Equality Act of 2010, for instance.

Be kind to yourself
Try not to put yourself down. Remember that this is going to be hard sometimes, so give yourself a break.

Relationships

Relationships can be a bit of a nightmare sometimes. Inevitably, relationships with family, friends and romantic partners affect everyone, but for us as trans people, there are once again additional layers and extra stuff we often have to deal with.

With any relationship it's worth thinking about what it gives you and what you give it in return. Sometimes the relationship can be very one-sided, and sometimes it can be more equal. It's worth thinking about these things, especially if you feel anxiety around that relationship.

Let's take romantic relationships, for instance. Things that kept coming up for me when I was dating were things like:

- Where do I even begin to find someone?

- Who do I find attractive?

- Will they see me as trans first before they see the other parts of me?

- Should I tell people I'm trans first? Is this something they'll know already from seeing me or do I need to voice it?

- If I do, then when?

- How do I stay safe?

- How am I going to cope with the transphobia I'm going to experience while dating?

· Why am I even doing this?

All of these questions, and more, became regular thoughts for me and, it goes without saying, they brought with them a whole heap of anxiety.

If I'm honest, every time I've been single I've also been a bit of a mess. It's not been easy, and coupled with the fact that I'm trans, and also getting older every time I am single, it often feels like my anxiety gets out of control and unmanageable on a regular basis. Something I learnt from this, though, was that if it feels like you're only getting anxiety from a relationship, or even just from finding one in the first place, then it's okay to take a break for a while.

Like so much to do with anxiety, it helps to break things down a little. I found that a lot of my worries about dating were unfounded, or not as extreme as I thought they were. For a long time, I thought that being trans made me undatable. It was only when my therapist pointed out that I did keep going on dates, even though they didn't always work out, that I realized my perception of what was happening was very skewed to the negative, and I started to re-evaluate what was going on.

I'm not going to go into too much detail here because that's a whole other can of worms. Basically, my anxiety, my threat response, was kicking in too much. I expected cis people to react badly to me because of my transness, so when that happened it just confirmed my narrative that all my dating exploits were terrible because of my trans identity.

Any good experiences or experiences where my transness didn't matter just became something I ignored or relabelled as sympathy dates.

Thinking about this some more and talking about it with other people really helped me work through a lot of the anxiety I was feeling, and also helped me focus more on what I wanted.

I worked out that one-night stands made me anxious, for example, because I didn't like the ambiguity of them. They confused me because I enjoyed them in the moment, but then felt awful the morning afterwards. Once I understood this, then it meant that I was able to also understand more about what I was looking for when it came to dating.

When it comes to any relationship, be that romantic or otherwise, there's another really important thing to know (it's kind of the key thing in many ways and well worth exploring): if you don't know what you want, then it's going to be confusing and anxiety-inducing.

Here are some more things that I found helpful to think about.

Do a regular reality check

It's easy to see what you want to see, so it's worth doing a quick reality check from time to time. Think about what's bothering you, what's making you anxious about a particular relationship, or lack of, and try and compare your preconceptions of it with the reality.

If you find it tricky to do this, then ask a close friend for their honest perspective on the situation and see if it matches up with yours or not. Sometimes things are how you see them, but equally, sometimes they're not; and if it does prove to be the latter case, then that gives you a new starting point for further exploration.

Be honest with yourself

It's tough to be honest, but it can help a lot with anxiety and knowing what to do about it. If dating is making you feel anxious, it's important to honestly ask yourself, 'What am I getting from this?' If all it's doing is making you feel awful, then maybe it's time to stop doing it for a while.

Nothing is permanent – you always have a choice

For me, this really struck home when I was in a relationship that just wasn't working. In hindsight, we should have broken up a long time before we did, but we didn't because I thought that this was it. If we broke up, my life would be over and I'd never get a chance to be in a relationship again. I was literally in the last chance saloon.

The thing is, though, I wasn't being honest with myself, and I wasn't reality checking at all, in part because I was so anxious all the time that my brain just got fixated on that. It actually took someone else to point out that I did have options, even if they didn't seem ideal at the time.

Unsurprisingly, once I made a choice to break up, my anxiety lessened and I felt a lot better. If it's hard to see the choices you have, then, again, ask a close friend for their perspective. Sometimes you can be too close to something to see the full picture, which is when other people can be of enormous help, be they friends, therapists or family.

Don't do yourself down

A lot of people out there are going to try and put you down, and a lot of the time it's going to be very linked to your trans identity. I don't get why people do this, but they will do it regardless. These people really suck.

Want to know who doesn't suck?

You!

So, don't do yourself down. Try to be as kind to yourself as possible, even when it feels like an impossible thing to do. Look at it this way. There are plenty of people out there being horrible to trans people already, so the best thing you can do to push back against this is be kind to yourself. If you can find even one thing you like about who you are, then that's one less thing to feel anxious about, which can only be a win in my book.

On Anxiety – Maeve

What does anxiety look and feel like for you?
Anxiety is an engine bolted into the heart of me. It's like an old motorbike travelling at speed. Sometimes it rattles me to my core and I feel like I'm going to come apart and strew pieces of myself all over the road. Sometimes it shakes and vibrates me in such a way that my whole being slides into tune with it and I become anxiety. White noise. It's like flying. Watching myself from inside a screaming hell.

Anxiety to me kind of feels like a by-product of wanting. Like, I want to know what's going on, what something is, what it means, what's going to happen, what's expected of me, where to go, and so on, but there's a ratio of want/get which is kind of like a see-saw.

So, in order to get something, you need to do a certain amount of wanting, right? The correct amount of wanting will spur you on to go get the thing you want. It will inspire you to do the necessary tasks. Wanting is not enough on its own but it is a catalyst. Sometimes you can pull something to you just by wanting, but that's a different conversation. However, if your want ratio is higher than the get ratio, you're revving hard but you're in a low gear, banging on the door but there's no answer.

If you want something which it is just not possible to have, then that creates a surplus energy. That energy is anxiety... I need to know what's happening but I need that more than it is possible for me to get the knowledge I want. I need to leave this place but social norms dictate that I must stay and be seen to be enjoying myself. I become anxious.

Anxiety robs me of time. It stops me from feeling connected with the present moment and instead plunges me into a current of uncertainty which is enough to freeze me in a dissociated state, sometimes for days and weeks on end. I can't think my way out of a loop of doubt and fear.

How has anxiety impacted your life and the way you live?
I've always been anxious, I know that now, but it was not always apparent to me. I recently learned that I have ADHD [attention deficit hyperactivity disorder] and that I'm autistic, and both of these revelations have had a profound influence on my understanding of anxiety. For the longest time I felt like I was fundamentally broken. Worried about how worried I was, over and over for ever amen. I couldn't tell what it was about me that set me apart from other people but I knew it was real. I internalized a lot and blamed my latent queerness and the fact that I wanted to be a girl. I started to hate myself for being tired all the time and frightened of people and I became anxious. I became hyperaware.

I always know where the exits are, I am constantly assessing people for threat. I can hear everything which is going on ALL the time. I can see the air moving and feel the most subtle changes in the environment. My body is hypermobile, so on a sort of sub-level I am concentrating on my balance, my posture, pain in my joints and battling against fatigue. I am sensitive to light and I see the tiniest movements, notice reflections and am often caught like a headlight rabbit by glares of light. I see pattern and form in everything and I see numbers and words and feelings as colours. I can see people's emotions radiating around and off them and I can project myself to any point in the world and imagine what it must be like there so vividly that I might as well be there. Sometimes it happens when I don't want it to and I find myself sucked into a news story or a film and I am there. In the riot. At the scene of the murder or in the war.

I can feel time swirling around me and I know that it moves differently depending on where you are in relation to it. My mind runs constantly and I am plotting my escape. I have schemes and plans and designs forming and revising and re-forming constantly and ALL of what I am describing happens ALL the time. I have not found a way to make it stop or even really slow down much and I'm confident that my anxiety is born out of this constant barrage of stimulus which I am trying to process on the fly while also attempting to pass as a functioning 'normal' adult human.

What helps you when it comes to your anxiety?
I find that it helps to give voice to my anxiety. We converse quite a lot and it looks a bit like this...

Anxiety

You took my younger years and

Helped me piss them up the wall.

Snort them along cisterns to the horizon and back.

No regard at all, for accumulating capital or securing some sound safety.

Things which would help to eliminate you.

What's there to prepare for when the future is just broken
glass all over everything?

Everybody's best pal

Always there with a joke and a hollowed-out heart. Dying.

Up all night ruminating under la lune

Last one home holding hands with the moon

And riding cold sheets as the sun comes up

Lost lonely, lazy lying to my family

And fearful that I might die.

Pin me to my bed

And stare into my eye

Loose my heart of your strangle hold and let me roam free

Anxiety

Let me be.

CHAPTER 8

Medical Services and How to Cope with Them

This is a big one for a lot of us, and it can be a major cause of anxiety. How medical services work for trans people is going to vary depending on where you are. I'm in the UK, so a lot of my experiences are based around the NHS, and going private, but there are also some general things to think about across the board wherever you are.

One of the first things I asked myself, in relation to accessing trans health care, was 'Do I trust in the system, and risk facing potential gatekeeping if the clinicians hear something they don't like, or do I say what I think they want to hear, and hopefully get the health care I'm after?'

Ultimately, this is always going to be a personal choice and it is also very dependent on where you live (different places have very different approaches to trans health care, ranging from okay to non-existent) and what resources, both personally and externally, you have available to you.

Here is what I did. I first accessed gender identity services via the NHS in the UK in 2007, when things were quite different to how they are now. There was still a waiting list at that time, but it was months rather than years. I think I had to wait about six months to be seen, which seems like nothing in comparison with nowadays, although to me it still felt like a long time.

Back then you had to have a psychiatric assessment before you could be seen (thankfully, this is no longer normally the case in the UK). Basically, you'd get an appointment with a psychiatrist, who would grill you about everything. This would include your entire life history, relationships, your family, sex life and, hilariously, preferences, because clearly who you find attractive is a big factor in if you're trans (it's not, obviously).

I was reasonably honest with the psychiatrist, although I also made sure to word how I spoke about my transness in a very definite and sure way. From reading about other people's experiences, I knew that if I showed anything that could be perceived as doubt about this, then it could impact on what happened next.

Rather rudely, in the written-up assessment of this session I was described as making a 'rather unremarkable woman'. I like to think that this was some sort of reverse psychology to inspire me to become a 'remarkable woman', but jokes on the guy who wrote that, because I've steadfastly stuck to being as unremarkable as possible. Nobody tells me what to do.

Over the next few years, I had various appointments at the Gender Identity Clinic in London, got some speech therapy with an amazing doctor, and had the various hormones and surgeries I wanted. Overall, the process was pretty smooth, but throughout it all I was very aware of potential gatekeeping, so there were some things I didn't talk about because I feared that they would stop me from getting what I wanted.

I didn't ever mention that although I primarily identify as

female, there are aspects of who I am that feel more agender. I didn't talk about how my sexuality is actually quite fluid and can fluctuate from pansexual, to lesbian, to asexual. I avoided using terms like 'genderqueer' or 'queer', even though sometimes I felt those labels work really well for me. I definitely down-played my mental health issues. I knew for a fact that hormones could be withheld if you showed too many signs of depression or anxiety, even though one of the main reasons I was depressed and anxious was because I wasn't on hormones.

The way I looked at it was that there were things that I needed in order to carry on existing in this world. There was a way to get these things but it involved jumping through some hoops. Sure, jumping through those hoops meant that I had to say what people wanted to hear in order to tick some boxes that said this person is trans. And sure this is not a great system, but it is the system we have, and I wasn't prepared to sacrifice my wellbeing to fight that system whilst I was in it. Some people may feel differently, and I'm not saying this is the right way to approach this, just that this is how I did it. We all have different experiences and different approaches, so it's important to work out what's best for you.

So how is it different now in the UK? Well, the waiting list is much, much longer. As I write this, we are in the middle of the Covid-19 crisis, so the waiting time is only going to get worse as the NHS recovers from this worldwide pandemic. Sadly, most people accessing NHS services are potentially looking at a minimum 2–3-year waiting list. Waiting times between ap-pointments can be months or even years, as the system is hugely oversubscribed and massively understaffed. There are certain surgeries as well that are not currently accessible on the NHS. For example, facial feminisation surgery, breast implants, voice pitch surgery and hair transplants are not routinely available.[1] This means that for many people, going private is something they have to think about very seriously. This, of course, comes with its own problems. Private services are oversubscribed as well, so there is still a period of waiting, although it is much shorter. The biggest problem of course is the cost. Surgery through private health care is incredibly expensive – we're talking thousands, sometimes tens of thousands of pounds, which most of us don't have.

We've spoken about surgeries earlier in this book, so jumping back to that for a moment, I recently had some FFS. I went abroad to a clinic in Spain to have it done, and it cost me roughly £16,000. This was for a rhinoplasty and some forehead reconstruction. I raised the money via credit cards, saving for many years and some incredible generosity from my partner and our families. Doing this was one of the best things I've done for myself and it's helped in so many ways, but also, it was one of the most anxiety-inducing things I've ever done. Trying to raise all that money, which until recently was more money than I earnt in a year, was terrifying and grim, and I still don't quite believe I did it.

In many parts of the world the only option you have for trans health care is to go private. Some places have health insurance that will cover the cost, but other places don't. In some countries there just isn't any care at all, because trans people aren't recognized as being real.

It's not easy to access health care related to your trans identity, be that surgeries, hormones or mental health services. There is a lot of gatekeeping, and surgeries can become ridiculously

---

1   NHS UK (2020) 'Gender dysphoria.' Available at https://www.nhs.uk/conditions/gender-dysphoria/treatment.

expensive very quickly. All of this is hugely anxiety-inducing as well, just to really rub it in.

Things that can help when accessing trans health care

What can we do to help mitigate all this anxiety? How can our anxiety levels be managed, especially when it can feel pretty hopeless because of the costs and time involved? Below I've written down some of the things that helped me. As previously mentioned, some of these suggestions might work better than others for you; tackling anxiety is all about finding what suits you as an individual.

Plan

Making a plan is often helpful. Think about what you want. Is it surgery? Hormones? For someone to just believe what you're saying? All of the above and more?

Work it out and write it down. Things to think about for your plan are:

- What would I want in an ideal world?

- What's realistic, both now and in the future?

- How long am I going to have to wait?

- What can I do to mitigate any anxiety between now and when I get what I need and want?

- What can I do now, and what will have to wait?

- How much is this going to cost?

Accept

This is a bitter pill to swallow, but there's a chance that some things are just not going to happen. Accepting this is a tough one because it's not fair and it sucks.

It's especially rough for us as trans people because some stuff is just how we are. For example, I'm never going to be petite. My bones, my body, what I am are tall. This makes me stand out, and even if I label it as being 'Amazonian', sometimes it still sucks.

It sucks that if you want trans-related surgery, there's always going to be a cost, be that time, money or pain. It can eat you up and heighten anxiety unless you accept that sadly this is the reality.

It's important to also know what to accept and what to fight against. If your doctor treats you badly and tries to gatekeep, for example, you shouldn't accept that. Complain, get a new doctor, ask around and find a trans-friendly one. It's about working out what's in your control and what's not.

You can't make a waiting list go faster but you can get ready for that day when you get to the top of it.

Talk to others

Talking is good. It's a way to find out about stuff, to get support and to make new friends. It helps ease anxiety as well, even if the idea of it doesn't always feel that way.

Especially when it comes to medical stuff to do with being trans, talking to others is an excellent way of getting useful information. For example, for years as part of my hormone therapy I'd been having an injection in my stomach every three months. Now injections are not my fave thing in the world, and injections in the stomach? Ooof. Not fun at all. It was only through talking to other trans people that I discovered there was a better drug I could take. I went to my endocrinologist and got changed over to a much better three-monthly injection, this time in the bum, which was also very preferable to tummy injections.

I don't think I'd have known about this unless I'd spoken to other trans people about what they were going through and what medication they were on.

Once you have more information, it's often easier to go to your doctor and get what you need, as being informed makes you feel more empowered, which can help ease some of the anxiety you may have.

Save

If you can, start saving. It's not going to be an option for everyone – it's only recently become an option for me, to be honest, and even then, it wasn't enough, but it did help a bit when it came to covering the cost of surgeries.

Distract yourself

Come up with things you can do to pass the time. This is helpful while you're waiting for things to happen, and also helpful when you're recovering from surgeries. Things rarely happen instantly. Most take time, and often that time is out of your control.

Do something to make that time go more quickly, to stop your anxious brain from kicking in and making things worse, and, most importantly, to feel better.

Sit and wait for this to pass, knowing that you're not alone

If it all gets too much, sometimes this is the only option you have. This will pass – it's inevitable. Time just keeps on flowing, and feelings will ebb and flow with it.

You may find that accessing trans health care comes in fits and starts. You'll see someone and feel like things are finally moving, only for it all to stop again for months at a time, making you feel like you're getting nowhere.

It is shit, this much I do know, but also you're not alone in this. It can feel like there are so many obstacles in your path. You might not have any money to pay for all the things you need, or you feel too awful or anxious to even start the process of speaking to a medical professional. You may have got onto a waiting list only to discover that it's two years long, or feel that no matter what you do, what surgeries you have or what hormones you take, you'll never be seen as your true gender.

All these things and more are things others have felt as well. These people are out there – hell, I'm one of them – so seek them out, talk to each other, and know that given time it will be okay.

Getting what we need from life is tough sometimes. It can seem stacked against us one moment and then really positive the next. It's unpredictable and challenging to navigate, and often pretty random.

It's also very anxiety-inducing.

There are things you can do to mitigate this though. It's not always easy, but it is worth it.

Things you can do to help manage your anxiety, and get what you need from life

Break it down into manageable chunks

If everything seems very overwhelming, then try to pause in order to work out what's going on. If you're trying to get a job at the same time as you're managing hormone doses, working out how to get the surgeries you desperately need and deciding what to eat for tea tonight, you are going to struggle. Break it down, work out what needs to happen first and start making a plan!

Know that some things can wait

If you're feeling anxious today, then sometimes the best thing you can do is just go with it. If it's a bad anxiety attack, then realistically you're not going to get stuff done, so roll with that and give yourself a break. It's sometimes easy to think that if you do this, then you're giving up or giving in. You're not. What you are doing is being kind to yourself; you're realizing that today isn't a good day, and that you need to practise some self-care.

If it can't wait, know that you've got this

Some things can't wait. Appointments with doctors or job interviews, for example, are things that are less with the 'I'll do it later' mindset. They're also, unfortunately, big on the anxiety.

If you feel your anxiety mounting, remember to breathe, say your mantras, walk around the block, scream into a pillow or do whatever it is that helps you manage this.

Remember that time will keep on flowing forwards, and that whatever it is that's causing you to feel this way will pass. Remember that you have got this. Remember that it might actually be a positive thing if you get that job or get the answers you need from the medical professional you're seeing.

Think about how in the future you're going to be so glad and so proud that you managed to do this thing.

You've got this.

On Anxiety – Meg-John (MJ)

What does anxiety look and feel like for you?

As for many trans and non-binary people, anxiety for me is highly related to trauma. What I used to label 'fear' or 'panic' I've now learned to label as an 'emotional flashback', from reading the literature on complex PTSD. This is like a regular flashback but it just consists of feelings, often without any memory accompanying them.

What happens is that something triggers my trauma response. It could be as big as a conflict or somebody overstepping my boundaries, or as small as a bad dream or my struggle to figure out what to watch on TV tonight! I feel anxious and, if I don't notice what's happening, it can quickly spiral into a very frightening place. It feels like going down the plug-hole of the sink. Once there, I feel like I'm in a life-or-death situation, I can't make any decisions, and everything becomes terrifying. Shame often accompanies it: the sense that I'm a bad or broken person.

This experience also relates to smaller anxiety feelings – like worries – which are my way to try to predict anything frightening that might happen, in order to try to avoid being plunged into that terrifying place. Social anxiety and/or agoraphobia can also be related as they can be – again – about avoiding potentially triggering situations. But those approaches – of worry and avoidance – can lead to me becoming caught up in noisy thoughts a lot of the time, or my world shrinking so that more and more things become scary.

What do you do to feel better when you're feeling anxious?
I'm definitely in a process of trying to heal the underlying trauma: the cPTSD [complex post-traumatic stress disorder] and the traumatic times in my life since childhood which have retraumatized me. This is about learning to recognize our patterns and where they come from, particularly whether we tend to go into fight, fright, freeze or fawn coping mechanisms. For me it's often fawn, but also sometimes flight into things that offer short-term relief but are not helpful long-term, like

overwork or distracting. The theory is that many 'addictions' come from that place.

Therapy, journalling, sharing with other trans and non-binary people in similar situations, and spiritual practices all help me a lot to tackle this on an everyday basis.

When I'm actually going into an emotional flashback, there are many different things I try to do. Different things work on different occasions. If I can notice that I'm starting to feel anxious – or circling the plug-hole – sometimes it is enough to name that I'm at risk of a flashback, perhaps to another person, and recognize what the trigger was and remind myself that it isn't life-and-death even though it may feel like it. If I'm starting to sink, then it can be good to shake my body till I'm out of breath, ask a friend to talk me through it, put my head in cold water, breathe deeply, feel my body, or really notice the room I'm in in detail. This is all about grounding myself and reminding myself that I'm safe enough right now, because the brain and body feel as if they're back in a dangerous situation at these times.

If I've actually gone all the way into a flashback, then it can be best to do extremely soothing things like putting myself to bed with a safe book or TV show, fixing a hot chocolate, or asking a friend to hold me through it. Such times can last for days or longer, in which case going into extremely gentle mode for the duration is a good plan, remembering that it will end, however hard that is to believe.

If you had one piece of advice for another trans/non-binary person who's experiencing anxiety, what would it be?
I'd strongly suggest learning about cPTSD and getting some trauma-informed therapy if you can access it. cPTSD is so common in our community and it's often misdiagnosed as anxiety,

depression, or even borderline or other 'personality disorders'. My dear friend Alex Iantaffi has a great podcast on trans and cPTSD on their Gender Stories podcast, which is a really helpful starting place. Pete Walker's book on cPTSD and Sarah Peynton's *Your Resonant Self* are also super-helpful resources [see Further Reading and Resources].

CHAPTER 9

Finding Joy

There are some things that we do that are intrinsically seen as social things. They nearly always involve others, and more often than not the sharing of an activity makes it more enjoyable. Sometimes, though, just sometimes, a thought crosses my mind and I decide that I'd like to try something on my own.

I'm not talking big things here – just everyday stuff, like going to a restaurant, seeing a band, having a drink or going to the cinema. The things we usually do with other people.

This might seem counterintuitive when it comes to anxiety, but strangely I've found it very helpful in managing the anxiety symptoms that regularly occur in my life, and it's actually kind of rewarding and liberating.

Doing something simple at first, like going to the cinema on your own, can be really empowering and actually help with anxiety. Often, when I go to the cinema with friends, I feel a pressure and my mind starts thinking about how they feel and whether they're enjoying the film or not. (Incidentally, this anxiety grows exponentially if the film we are seeing is one I've suggested.)

If I'm struggling with being around too many people, it can

become amplified because I'm with a group and the social pressure can get a bit much. On my own, though, it's a different story. All that anxiety is washed away, and suddenly I can just focus on my experience. Suddenly I am free.

I love that my local cinema sells home-made cakes. I love that you can buy a cup of tea and take it into the room where they show the film. It feels like the most exciting thing, like settling down in front of the telly at home, except the telly has grown huge and is now in an enormous, dark room that smells of popcorn.

I love going to the cinema in the daytime, because it feels like I'm skipping work, even when I'm not. On those rare occasions when it's just me in the cinema, it feels like a private showing, and it feels special. When I go through the doors and there's no one else there, my heart sometimes skips a beat because I know there's a chance that this magical event might happen today.

I love the sound. I love how loud it is. I love how it makes my bones vibrate and my heart squeeze tight. I love how I sometimes find myself holding my breath as the glorious, enveloping noise covers me, like a crashing wave, overwhelming and yet fleeting, leaving me wishing for more.

You could get all this by going to the cinema with someone, and a shared thing can be something amazing, but there's a part of me that doesn't want to share this with someone. I want the hairs to stand up on my arms, my breath to become shallow and held, my eyes to feel like they can't take everything in fast enough, my ears to become numb with the sound. I want this, and I want this to be for me alone. I'm making time for myself, and not just any old time either – this is quality time. This is a joyful time.

For me going to the cinema alone is a joyful experience, and joy is an amazing antidote to anxiety. Finding something joyful feels like a difficult thing to do sometimes. 'Joy' is not even a word we use that much, but it is a powerful emotion.

Aside from my lone-person cinema trips, the last time I felt joy was from watching a video on the internet. It was a video someone had made on top of a snowy mountain just as the sun was rising, and it was honestly the most beautiful thing I'd seen in years.

There wasn't any commentary; it was just a panning view of a sunrise, set to a snowy backdrop. Something about it hit me hard and, I'm not going to lie, it brought a tear to my eye, not from sadness, but from joy.

As grown-ups we often don't have time to even think about joy; there's so much going on that takes up more time. As trans people, it can often feel like joy is something that's very distinctly missing in our lives, what with everything else that we experience.

If we're feeling anxious or have a long-term anxiety condition, then joy is often the last thing we'll feel, and even thinking about finding it can be a struggle. It's super-important, though, that we try.

Joy and its sister feeling, awe, are amazing feelings and can act to counter anxiety. Research has shown that feeling joyful lessens our chances of having a heart attack, lowers our cholesterol and decreases our stress and anxiety levels.

For me, going to the cinema on my own is a magical experience that eases my anxiety and will surely have a lasting effect on how I am in the future as well.

This works really well for me, but how do you find out what brings you joy? How do you overcome the obstacles that anxiety so deftly puts in your way?

Well, first, although it might feel like an impossible task, you can find joy for yourself, and you can overcome those obstacles.

I know this because I did. I know this because people I know did. All the evidence I have suggests that you too can do this.

Things that can help you find joy

I'm going to talk about a few things you can do to help with finding joy, and some related emotions, like hope. These exercises can be as complex or as simple as you like. Really go for it, or just dip your toe in. All these exercises work better if you do them semi-regularly, but equally they can be useful just as a starting point or a guide to something better.

Joy lists

A joy list is a list of ten things that bring you joy. These can be things that have brought you joy in the past or that will bring you joy in the future or that bring you joy right now. They can even be a mix of past, present and future; the key is to find ten things.

Here, to give an example, is my joy list, as it stands right now.

1. Going to my allotment, where I can grow things and get back to nature.

2. Going to the cinema in the daytime, on my own.

3. Playing Stardew Valley (a video game about farming).

4. Hearing the birds sing.

5. Going somewhere warm.

6. Baking.

7. Dancing.

8. Getting into bed in the evening (bonus points for putting on clean sheets first).

9. Hot baths.

10. Music.

Some of mine are very basic, and some require a little more effort, but they're all achievable, and all things I can fall back on if I need to.

Writing these things down also gives me a physical reminder on a piece of paper that I can use when I am feeling anxious or stressed.

If I'm feeling overwhelmed by work, I know that when I get home, if I have a bath or just go to bed and watch a film, it'll calm and soothe me, and potentially even bring me a degree of joy.

It's like a really simple life hack that you can keep on adding to, updating and using as your situation changes.

The perfect day

Imagine, for a moment, what your perfect day would look like.

It's a tough one to think about, I know, especially if you're also experiencing anxiety. It quite possibly feels like the very last thing you'd want to think about, in fact. This is one of the problems with anxiety. It doesn't like you to think about the perfect things. It's very much about the less than perfect, the stress and the fear. Honestly, it really just drags you down. And once you're down, it's incredibly hard to get up again.

Anxiety is a heavy weight to bear, and it's hard to feel like you can put it down and rest for a while. It's so important, though, to think about how things can be better, because that in turn gives you a roadmap for the future.

Writing down what your perfect day would look like gives

you pointers and clues to help you with anxiety. It doesn't need to be an in-depth description, unless you want it to be – it's your perfect day, you make the rules.

When you're writing about your perfect day, think about which things are new things you can aim for, and which are things you've already done and would like to do again. It's good to recognize that there are often going to be things you write down that have happened in the past and so are achievable. Why is that good? Because it gives you hope; and hope, like joy, is another amazing antidote to anxiety.

You might find at first that this is quite a difficult exercise to do. It's very tricky sometimes to see any positivity when you're feeling awful, but give it a go and see where you get to. If a whole day seems too much to write about, break it down to a morning, or an hour, or choose just one thing that you'd like in your perfect day and grow it from that.

Gratitude journal

Okay, I know. Gratitude journals? Really, Freiya? I know it's a bit cringy, especially if you're a big old cynic like me. But stick with me on this, because actually a gratitude journal can be an enormous help with anxiety.

A gratitude journal is a book or diary where you write down things that you're grateful for. Some people do this daily, others less frequently, but the idea is the same. You think about what you're happy and grateful for in your life. It could be as simple as having a cat, or as fancy as getting a promotion at work. The key thing is to try and think of something, even if it's as small as 'I managed to get dressed today.'

Gratitude journalling is great because it gives things perspective. If you're anxious, it's easy to feel like everything is awful. This sort of journalling gives a space to challenge that, in a gentle and kind way. It's very private. No one else needs to see this, and you don't need to tell anyone either, so it's a safe way of acknowledging your feelings whilst also trying to find something more positive to help lift those feelings up.

Here's an example from my own experiences with this.

A while back, I got shouted at whilst using a public toilet in an airport. It was because I was trans, and the person shouting at me decided that I was in the wrong toilet, even though I wasn't. For a lot of us, this is one of our worst nightmares and it's incredibly anxiety-inducing. I'm not going to lie; it shook me up big time. It happened at an airport as well, which for us as trans people often isn't the best place to be.

Dealing with something like this is horrible and upsetting, and it's very hard to not just fall to bits. What helped me was to think about the things I was grateful for. It sounds a bit meh, I know, but I'd just come back from a really peaceful holiday, so I just kept repeating in my head, 'You've had a lovely holiday, that's what matters. Don't let this person's ignorance ruin it.'

It also helped to think about the shitty life the person that shouted at me probably has, and maybe curse them a little (in my head, obvs). I don't think there's anything wrong in that, as long as it doesn't start consuming you.

Thinking about what I was grateful for gave me perspective, helped me cope and gave me strength. Sure, it did also make me cry and upset me, but I also got out of the anxiety this produced much more intact because there was something positive and joyful to counter the bad.

Keeping a gratitude journal isn't always an easy thing to do, but if you do manage to do it, it can provide some useful resources to fall back on if anxiety-inducing things happen out there in the wild.

Being kind and helping others

Being kind is amazingly good for us. Being kind to others releases feel-good hormones like serotonin, which make us feel better. It can help hugely with anxiety as well, as being kind boosts our mood, and makes us feel valid and worth something.

When you help other people, you also start thinking about them more as well, which helps you get outside of yourself and your own mind. We all know how easy it is to get bogged down in our own stuff, and how all-consuming it can become, so getting away from that can help a lot. Helping others can relieve symptoms of stress and anxiety, and in turn can give you new ways of coping when anxiety and stress come for you.

The other great thing about being kind and helping others is that it's mostly free. It's something we can all do, and it has an amazing knock-on effect. Our world can often be quite cold and isolating, but kindness can counter that.

Try and do one kind thing every day, even when the world isn't that kind to you. It is especially important for us as trans people to know kindness, because the world is often not that kind to us. If we can be kind, despite all the hate shown towards us, then we ultimately win. It may sound like a cliché, but our kindness is our strength. It helps us and it helps others, and that can only be a good thing.

Finding something that brings you joy, something that gives you hope for the future, something that just makes you feel okay – even if it's just for a while – is so important when it comes to managing anxiety.

If all you ever feel is anxious, then you're also going to feel like you can never get a break. Remembering that this isn't the whole truth, and that you can get a break, can be really liberating. Getting a break does also mean accepting that sometimes you're the only one with the power to actually make it happen, which in turn can make it extra difficult, but it is worth trying at least.

It's not always easy, but finding joy could be the best thing you do for yourself. Find yours and use it to make your life better.

On Anxiety – Effie

What does anxiety look and feel like for you?
In my experience, what anxiety looks and feels like has morphed and shifted over the last six or seven years and continues to do so now.

At first, it was an eruption. I think after years of suppressing depression or bingeing in unhealthy outlets to hide from it, something just snapped. My first panic attack felt violent. I remember being completely frozen, just sitting at the kitchen table of my student halls whilst my mind just kind of let go of me and all of my defences came tumbling down. It was terrifying, I had no idea what was happening to me.

This went on to set the tone of what anxiety would look like for a couple of years. Fear. It was fresh, unexpected and unpredictable. For a solid two years it really was all-consuming. Whenever I'd leave the house, I would panic. Sometimes I'd muster up the guts to get the bus somewhere and then be off and walking back home after two stops. I'd go to catch up with friends I'd ignored for months and leave after ten minutes. So, I gave up.

Anxiety's next phase for me was isolation, for the best part of 2–3 years. I stayed inside, I got high, and convinced myself I was okay. I really fell into a trap here. Anxiety wasn't fresh any more, but I'd resigned myself to it. I got comfortable with the strict boundaries I'd set to protect myself from it, which meant staying indoors, and keeping to myself. I look back on those years with a great amount of sadness. Not regret – I learnt a lot about myself during that period – but I damaged myself in ways I still haven't fully recuperated from.

Learning to live and exist in the world with anxiety has taken, and is taking, years. I don't know if it's something you can ever really get rid of. These days, I think of it as 'a dread', a little monster that clings to one of my feet everywhere I go, so I take it with me and occasionally it climbs up to my shoulder to speak into my ear and remind me it's still there. It's heavy and it's tiring, but I'm learning to live with it.

What do you do to feel better when you're feeling anxious?
If I'm at home, I take a nice, long shower. Since growing my hair out and discovering Lush products, there are few things I take more enjoyment in than washing my hair. Hair treatment, shampoo, conditioner and hair moisturizer. Come out feeling like a new woman. Then, camomile tea, vegan ice-cream (if I haven't already finished it), and Star Wars. Never underestimate the value of self-care, whatever that looks like to you.

If you had one piece of advice for another trans/non-binary person who's experiencing anxiety, what would it be?
Know that you can leave at any time. There is nowhere you *have* to be. A big trigger for my anxiety attacks was feeling like I had to be somewhere or sit still for more than 20 minutes. Cinemas, trains, presentations, queues, social events, you get the picture. But coming to the realization that if I want to leave, I can just leave, and being okay with that, made a world of difference.

Do I actually walk out of all of these places? Sometimes, yes, and that's okay! But if you truly believe you can leave at any time, the urgency to walk out is hugely diminished.

What one thing, above all others, helps you when it comes to your anxiety?

The support of the people closest to me. It's been a wild ride with anxiety, and it takes a lot of strength to open up about your triggers. I was embarrassed by a lot of the things I know will reduce the chances of me panicking, and the last thing I wanted was to 'make it someone else's problem'. But, ultimately, telling my friends and family enabled me to start comfortably doing the things I was avoiding again.

'Hey, when we go to the cinema, can I take the aisle seat in case I need to run away without disturbing any of the other cinema goers or in case I suddenly think I'm going to wet myself?'

'Yes, of course.'

It seems scary at first, but if the people you tell care about you (which they do, that's why you're telling them), it just becomes something they do. A couple of friends of mine bought me tickets to a comedy-show for my birthday last year. As I looked at the tickets, 'the dread' started creeping up until one of them said, 'We got good seats – nice and central with one on the aisle.'

Your friends are your allies. Ask for the support you know you would offer them.

How does being trans/non-binary affect your anxiety?

Anxiety broke me down. It was only by really losing sight of the person I had been that I could investigate who I actually was (and am) as I rebuilt myself.

Picture a vase that has fallen off of a table and smashed. Through the process of picking out every part of myself and putting the vase back together, I slowly came to terms with the realization and acceptance of the fact that I am trans. I have rebuilt the vase and analysed every piece of it. I am the same person, but with a better understanding of who that person is.

As a result, the self-acceptance of my transness and my queerness have been intrinsically linked to the journey of understanding my anxiety.

For me, any new anxieties that have arisen since being out, being seen and visible as trans, have largely revolved around safety. As a 6 foot 6 inches trans gal, I am very visible and I am always switched on. What if those guys start running towards me? Why's that man looking at me like that? I'm getting strong TERF [trans-exclusionary radical feminist] vibes off her... the list goes on.

The point is, I do not feel safe a lot of the time, and we can call that anxiety or we can call that fear or we can use a plethora of other words which will never quite encapsulate the trans experience. But I know it's something cis people will never fully understand, and I know that I see it in the eyes of my trans siblings.

We have always been here, and we will not be silenced, and me and my dread are proud to still be marching on, anxiety-ridden and queer as can be.

CHAPTER 10

Practical Things We Can Do

So, what other things can we do to help with our anxiety? Well, it turns out that we can do lots. I've mentioned quite a few things already, but in this chapter we'll take a look at a few more anxiety-busting options.

Of course, once you know what to do, there's the issue of then actually putting it into practice. Unfortunately, anxiety is a bit of a limiter when it comes to actually doing things, because it is all about warning us of the dangers of doing anything and everything. After a while this gets really tiring and wears you down.

Even when you do get the strength and the courage to actually do something, there's still all the other stuff, like can I actually afford to do this? It's all very well saying I should go get some therapy, but therapy costs money, which is something I don't always have. Even if you do have money, there's a good chance that you're saving it for trans-related things, like surgeries, medical expenses or any of the many things that we as trans people need to actually survive.

For me personally, when it comes to money, trans stuff takes priority. When I only had enough money to pay for electrolysis or therapy, the choice was simple. Having the hair removed from my face would have an instant positive effect on my dysphoria, whereas therapy would take months, possibly years before there was any payoff.

And what about finding the time to do all this as well? Depending on your circumstances, time might be very limited, or you might have loads. If you're working six days a week in a busy job, chances are you're going to be wiped by the time you actually have some time for yourself, so you might not feel like going for a long walk up a mountain.

If you've got a side gig (be that writing books, working in a bar or handing out leaflets to passers-by at the weekend) because you need two jobs to actually afford to live in these expensive times, then you're going to be done in by the time the evening comes round.

With this in mind, I've tried splitting these solutions into free things and things that cost more, time-consuming things and quick hits. I've been a worshipper of the gods of procrastination for a long time, so a lot of these are from my own experiences, but I've also asked around, so some come from others as well.

Some of these possibilities may seem simple, almost too simple. You may be thinking, well if it's that easy, why doesn't everyone do it? Sometimes, though, even easy things can be hard to actually do, especially if you're anxious or depressed. Also, we're sort of led to believe that solutions have to be difficult for them to be effective. Our society is often very focused on you having to put the work in to achieve anything, and mental health is no exception. To a degree, this is true – you need to make some sort of effort and you need to want things to get better in order to help improve your situation – but also, some things just are really simple, and really effective. Going for a walk in natural surroundings sounds pretty basic, but it's also a great and simple way to help make you feel better.

As you read through these ideas, some of them may seem contradictory; for instance, how can both staying connected with others and spending time alone work for anxiety? Well, what works for one person at a particular time might not for someone else. Part of tackling your anxiety is getting to know who you are and how you work. If you can start to understand more about yourself, you'll also be better informed about what might work for you in a particular situation, which can only be a good thing. It's all about stocking up that anxiety toolkit with the tools you need. Those tools are going to be different for every one of us, because we all differ in how we see things, in our life experiences and in how we manage our anxiety.

Quick things

The following are quick and easy fixes for when you're in a spot and need something to help you out right away.

Dance breaks

If you have a private space, then take a dance break. Dancing when there's no one watching is a cliché, but it's also a very good way of helping to overcome anxiety. It's freeing to move your body however you choose to, without judgement from others. It distracts your brain, burns up some energy and can help break a downward spiral. Find a song you want to dance to and make your own private disco!

Mindfulness

Mindfulness is something we hear a lot about nowadays. It's all about being in the moment, listening, looking, sensing what's around us, and focusing on what we're doing, and where we are. It's a little like meditation, and can be an amazing antidote to the overwhelming nature of our world. It's great because it's something we all have the ability to do as well, as we all have the capacity to be present; it just sometimes takes a bit of practice.

Being mindful doesn't have to be a big thing. There's lots we can do if we only have a little bit of time and need some sweet relief.

- *Colouring in:* There are a lot of adult colouring-in books about nowadays, and with good reason, because colouring-in helps to calm our anxious brains. Research in 2005 found that colouring in mandalas helped reduce anxiety, in part because of the focus and the meditative state it produced in the participants.[1]

- *Go for a walk:* This is frequently recommended when it comes to managing anxiety through mindfulness. By noticing how your body feels when you walk, and being present in the sensations around you, be that the birds singing, the breeze on your skin, or the smell of the coffee shop you're passing by, for instance, then in theory you'll also be practising mindfulness. It can be really helpful, as long as your walk doesn't put you in situations that may increase your anxiety. We've spoken about this earlier, and I'll talk about it some more in the next section, but going for a walk outside might mean we trans people end up getting more anxious because of how others behave towards us. It's difficult, but if you feel safe and are able

---

1   Curry, N.A. and Kasser, T. (2005) 'Can coloring mandalas reduce anxiety?' Available at https://files.eric.ed.gov/fulltext/EJ688443.pdf.

to, walking, even if it's just for five minutes round the block, can help.

· *Make a cup of tea:* Focus on the whole process, the smells, the colours, the warmth of the cup in your hands. Try to feel each sensation as you make the tea, and calm your mind. Of course it doesn't have to be a cup of tea either, the trick here is finding one thing that doesn't take that long to do, and focus yourself on that task. This will help give your mind something other than anxiety to think about, and hopefully distract it enough for the anxiety to lessen, or even pass.

Letting it all out

Sometimes things are just a bit shit. Anxiety can build up inside you and fill up, like a volcano waiting to pop, and you need a way to let it out. Finding a way to do this can be extremely helpful. Maybe it's screaming into a pillow, maybe it's just swearing for five minutes, or running round the block. Maybe it's taking a long hot bath and letting that anxiety melt away in the heat, or shaking it out from your head to your toes.

Finding something funny can be a great reliever of anxiety. It could be watching something funny online, or your fave show, or setting up an obstacle course for your cat, for instance.

If you can find an easy, safe way of letting it out then it can be very helpful in a push.

Reality check

Reality checking can be really useful when it comes to anxious thoughts. Anxiety can often create a distorted reality, messing with how we process the things around us. Reality checking focuses our mind on what's causing us anxiety (anxiety about being attacked by bears might be justified if they're lurking in the woods you're in, but that's not usually a danger we face in our modern, more bear-free world).

Reality checking is about breaking free from this distorted view and seeing what's actually going on. Breaking free is sometimes hard, because your brain is in anxiety mode, shutting off a lot of the thoughts that would normally challenge this. To help with getting past this block, people often use techniques such as cold water on their hands or face, pinching themselves or various counting techniques, like the 555 method, which I'll talk about in a bit.

Once you've broken free, you can assess the situation, challenge what you're feeling and see if the anxiety is valid (as in the case of the bear) or disproportionate. The great thing about this is the more you do it, the better you'll get at it.

Give yourself a break

It's important sometimes to just give yourself a break. This can be something as simple as looking out of the window for ten minutes or going to bed for the day, but the key is to try and cut yourself some slack. Anxiety is very consuming and it doesn't always leave you time or energy to just be still for a moment.

It's okay to say to yourself, 'I just need a break for a minute.' By telling yourself this, out loud or in your head, you're enabling yourself to do exactly that. Tell yourself that you know your anxieties won't magically vanish, but that you just need a little time to not have to worry about them right now.

You're not ignoring any worries or anxieties, but rather putting them on hold whilst you catch your breath. If it's difficult to do this, there are some practical ways you can give yourself a break as well.

- *Stretching:* Having a good stretch connects us with our bodies and occupies our minds in a very gentle way. It feels good, and you can also combine it with shaking your hands and feet, to literally shake out the tension within your body. Exhaling as you stretch can also help with regulating heart rate and stress levels.

- *Do something else:* Sometimes with anxiety we get stuck in that moment and we need a distraction. This distraction can act as a way of giving yourself a break. It can be whatever works for you, be that walking, taking a shower or bath, playing a video game, or reading, for example. Of course, the hard thing is finding out what works for you, so try out some different things, take a break, and don't feel guilty about doing it. This is self-care on your terms.

Just leave

Here's something that took me way too long to realize. If something, a situation or a place, is making me anxious I can just leave. I don't have to stay if it's making me uncomfortable. I know that for me, and maybe for you as well, some of my anxiety is informed by what I've been told is unacceptable. Society tells me that to leave a date, or party, or lunch date, or whatever, is rude, and that I should put others before myself and just suck it up.

This, though, doesn't account for how horrific anxiety can be. It doesn't account for how it makes us feel, or how it can make others feel. In other situations, if you were having a bad time, you'd stop doing that thing, so why should this be any different? I know I'm generalizing here to make a point, and sometimes it's not always as simple as just going, but also, just having that thought, knowing that you have that option, can be really freeing.

I remember a few years ago I went through a phase of going out in the evening to clubs and bars on my own. It was partly a sort of exposure therapy for my anxiety, and partly because I wanted to go out but didn't have anyone I could do that with. It was often quite intense, but one of the things that helped me overcome the anxiety I felt was knowing that I could just leave. I'd often stand outside the place I was going to and repeat 'I can just leave if it's bad' a few times, like a mantra, before I took the plunge. Sometimes, if it was bad, I would do just that.

It's a powerful thing to remember, and it can give you back some degree of control in situations that feel difficult or challenging.

Free things

Sunsets, sunrises and nature

The world around us is a very beautiful place. Sometimes it's easy to forget this, especially when you're suffering from anxiety and the world feels unsafe and unwelcoming.

It can be helpful to spend some time in nature, even if it's doing something as simple as watching the sun rise or set.

There's something very meditative about sunrises and sunsets, and here's a thing. Did you know that they're actually good for our mental health?

For real.

Watching the sun set or rise can calm us. It stimulates serotonin production and can catch you in a moment, grounding you and putting a pause on your busy brain.

Being in nature also has this effect, and even just a walk around your local park can be very helpful in clearing your head.

For me personally, when it comes to anxiety, I get very easily bogged down in my own mind. It becomes overwhelming and oppressive, almost inescapable, like this heavy cloud on my shoulders.

If I can muster myself to get outside, it can really help lift this feeling. It's not easy to do, as often anxiety will try to stop me from going out, but if I can break through, it does help a lot.

Sunlight helps me feel connected to myself. The warmth on my skin is something tangible I can feel, and walking connects me to my body because I can feel it when I move. It distracts me from what I'm feeling, because outside is full of stimulation.

I find that getting out into green spaces helps as the colour green, especially, is soothing for my little anxious brain.

Find a mantra/encouraging statement

This can be as simple or complex as you like. You just need something you can remember that you can then repeat in your head if you need it.

For example, I sometimes have panic attacks. My limbs start to feel like lead weights, and if I'm lying down it feels like I'm sinking into the floor. My heart rate goes up, my breathing gets messy and it feels like I'm in big trouble. At first it was pretty horrible as I had no idea what was going on, and I felt like I had no control over it at all.

I learnt, though, that actually I did have control over it; it just wasn't in the way I thought. I'd been focusing on trying to stop the panic attack, when in fact I just needed to let it happen.

To help with this I developed a simple mantra: 'This will pass in time.' I found that just repeating this, either in my head or quietly under my breath, really helped. It calmed me, it soothed me and it reassured me because it reaffirmed the truth I already knew: that this will pass in time. Now I use this mantra every time I feel anxious, or in a situation that I find challenging.

Sometimes mantras can be situation-specific as well. Another favourite of mine is 'You can just leave if you're not enjoying yourself,' something we spoke about earlier. This one obviously is more in relation to social anxiety, but again it's the repeated reassurance that helps. It's giving you back power and control in a situation where often that's the last thing you feel.

Mantras are very person-specific. You might want something as simple as 'I'm amazing' or something more detailed, like 'I'm amazing because...' The trick is finding the words that work for you.

Here are some more examples to help you get started:

- *'Other people feel this too'*: You are not alone in these feelings; others are having then right now, and will continue to do so in the future. Anxiety can be very isolating, so it's helpful to know you're not alone.

- *'This is only a paper tiger'*: 'Paper tiger' is an English translation of the Chinese phrase *zhilaohu* (纸老虎／紙老虎). It refers to something that feels very threatening, like a tiger, that upon closer inspection actually isn't. The phrase became better known after it was used by Mao Zedong, the leader of China, in various interviews in the 1940s and 50s. In these interviews he was using it in reference to American imperialism, but it's also a useful thing to remember in relation to anxiety. Often, once we stop and take a look at what is causing us anxiety, it will turn out to be a paper tiger, so it's a useful thing to try and remember!

- *'Cross bridges when you come to them'*: It's easy to feel anxious about the future. The future is naturally anxiety-inducing because it hasn't happened yet, and as trans people our future often feels incredibly uncertain, be that to do with work, surgery, identity or any other number of things. It's important to remember that a lot of these worries are in your mind right now, and it might be that they may never materialize. It's good to plan and think about what may happen, but when a worry becomes all-consuming, it can become out of proportion to the reality of the situation. Sometimes it's good to remind yourself that you can deal with what happens when it happens, rather than worrying about it right now. Plan for potential negative outcomes, sure, but remember that there may well be positive ones as well.

- *'Don't give up, you're doing okay'*: Perspective is everything. It's often helpful if you're feeling awful to think about how far you've come and to just say something to soothe yourself.

Talk to someone who gets it/stay connected

Talking to someone you trust can be helpful, especially if they have some level of understanding around the issues and experiences you've had.

Anxiety can make you feel pretty isolated, which isn't always the best thing for us. Sometimes connecting with someone can help, even if it's just to say, 'I'm feeling anxious, so I'm going to go and chill out for a bit on my own.'

Just vocalizing how you feel to someone can make a difference. They don't need to do anything; it's more about just having someone knowing how you're feeling and sharing that load. It's also helpful to say what you're going to do (for instance, 'I'm going to go and chill out in my room for a bit'), because it shows you're taking back some control over the anxiety you're feeling. You're saying, 'I got this, but I also wanted to let you know as well.'

555/54321 techniques

There are quite a few things you can do if you're feeling anxious and overwhelmed but don't want to go anywhere. The two most well-known ones involve counting and are sometimes known as the 555 technique and the 54321 technique.

Here's how they work:

- *555 technique:* The idea with this is to help root you in the moment and get you outside of your mind a bit. You can mix it up if you want, but here's the basic version to start with:
    - Find five things you can see. Focus on each one, thinking about the form, colour and shape.
    - Listen to five things you can hear. Think about where the sound is coming from, what it is and how loud or quiet it is.
    - Find five things you can touch. Feel them and think about what you're feeling: the textures, the actual object, the sensations that come with it.

- *54321 technique:* Again, this is an exercise to help focus your mind and quell racing thoughts. It helps your brain to calm itself and gives it a direction to go in that's not anxiety-based.
    - Find five things you can see.
    - Find four things you can feel.
    - Find three things you can hear.
    - Find two things you can smell.
    - Find one thing you can taste.

Again, you can mix these up if you want. The trick is to focus on each thing and distract your anxious brain. You can make a lot of variations with this basic model. Some people will forget the counting aspect and just focus on the colours of everything they can see, right down to the tiniest detail. Others will taste something and then try and describe all the different tastes they experience. Find what works for you and give it a go.

Spend some time alone

We looked at this in more depth earlier on in the book, but it's worth repeating. Hanging out on your own sounds like the worst thing to do when it comes to anxiety, but actually it can be very beneficial, especially if your anxiety is being driven by other people. Having a private, safe space you can go to, where you can just relax, catch yourself a bit, and deal with the anxiety you're feeling, without having to worry about anyone else, is really important.

For me, alone time is one of the most powerful tools I have for dealing with anxiety issues, and I often think of it like having a sanctuary away from the rest of the world. I make it my own space and it's a place I guard very carefully as well.

If you don't have a space you can make your own, then equally you can find some space by going for a walk with your headphones on, or even just sitting in your bathroom for a while. If it feels awkward, run the shower or have a bath.

Having a bath is a great way to relax and manage anxiety. Hot water can be very soothing; and if you have a particular scent you like, then some essential oils or scented bath bombs in the water can really lift your mood. Lavender, lemon/citrus scents, ylang ylang, rose, bergamot and neroli are all scents that are said to help with anxiety and stress.

Get a routine

Having a schedule or a system can really help with anxiety. It gives you a focus, a distraction and a purpose. It can be basic – something as simple as your morning routine or having a bath on Thursday night – but it's good to try and make it consistent and regular. Knowing there's this thing you do at a particular time can be grounding as well, and that can be vital if everything else feels chaotic and unmanageable.

This is just a memory

Sometimes when we feel anxiety, it can be helpful to remember that what we're actually feeling is a memory or echo from the past. When I'm walking down the street and I feel anxious in case someone starts on me, there's the very real threat that it might happen, but there are also all the experiences of that happening in the past weighing down on that. It's an extra load that you don't always need to carry, so it can be helpful to remind yourself that some of what you feel has already happened, and although it feels like it can still hurt you, it is something you can start to have some control over.

Memories can be powerful and distressing, but you can get control over them and use them to inform rather than hurt. This isn't easy and it often involves some degree of therapy, but it is something that has helped me in making anxiety-inducing situations more manageable.

Practise breathing/breath control/meditation

There are a lot – and I mean a lot – of resources out there for breathing and meditation exercises. Whole books are written about them all.

Like so much of this stuff, half the battle is finding out a routine that works for you. That will involve a little bit of trial and error, along with a hefty dose of research.

Here, as a starting point, is a simple breathing exercise:

1. Find a quiet and calm space, and sit, with your back as straight as possible and your eyes shut. (I have also tried this lying down. The important thing is to try and be as comfortable as you can be. I sometimes use cushions to prop myself up if I'm really tired!)

2. With your eyes closed, start thinking about your breathing. Breathe in and out through your nostrils, just as you would normally, thinking about the sensation and feeling of the air as it flows in and out of your nose.

3. Put one hand on your belly, and feel it move as you breathe. Put your other hand on your chest, and again feel it rise and fall as you breathe in and out. Some people will count their breaths in and out, like taking a deep breath and counting to four, then holding it for three, and then exhaling again for a count of four. Try and breathe from your stomach, as this is where calming breath comes from. When you're feeling anxiety, your breathing comes from your chest, which is not what we want here!

4. If your mind tries to wander, it's okay and it's totally normal, but try and bring it back to focusing on your breathing, in and out. Sometimes it can be helpful to have an inner monologue with your brain when it wanders off. For example, 'I know you think you want to think about that, but let's leave it for now, and listen, and feel our breathing some more. There will be time later for other things.'

5. Keep repeating the breathing, and the feeling of your breath until you start to feel calm.

Go for a walk

I want to talk about this separately, even though it forms part of a few other ways of dealing with anxiety, just because going for a walk has extra issues for us as trans people. Sometimes, for us, doing this to help with anxiety can actually add to anxiety, because going outside can mean that other people may harass you, because you're trans.

There is a lot of evidence to suggest that walking is great for anxiety: it lowers your heart rate; it distracts you from what's on your mind because of external stimulation; and if you walk somewhere scenic or pretty that can help as well.

So how can we get these benefits without also putting ourselves in potentially anxiety-inducing situations because of our trans identities?

Well, first, it goes without saying that we shouldn't have to deal with these sorts of problems. It's pretty awful that so many of us have to think about how to stay safe when all we want to do is go for a walk. There are no perfect solutions to this either, but there are some things we can do to help mitigate some of these anxieties.

- Get to know your neighbourhood. Think about where it's safe to walk and, more importantly, where you feel safe to walk.

- Consider ways you might become 'invisible'. Sometimes I deliberately wear what I call 'safe clothes' if I want to go for a walk without being hassled. For me this means a pair of jeans and a hoodie, although it might mean something else for you. I fully acknowledge that this is not ideal. We shouldn't have to censor how we look, just to be able to walk safely down the street, and it is terrible that this is a thing, but we're not alone in it. I know a lot of cis women that also have made the decision to do this, to feel safer and help reduce the levels of misogyny and sexism they experience on the street. Obviously, this isn't great on a societal level, but sometimes you just want to go for a walk without someone hating on you, and for me this is a compromise I've decided to make – for now, anyhow. It's a very personal thing, and for some people this won't be a path they want to take, but it is an option, and I feel it's important to put it out there. Sometimes not all the choices we have are ideal, so then it's a case of working out which ones work best for you.

- Walk with your friends or family or loved ones. I feel safer when I'm with someone, because it feels like I've got back-up. People are less likely to give me trouble if I'm with someone else; but if they do, there's someone with me to help out, stand up for me or get me somewhere safe. It's good to have someone that understands what you can potentially experience, so that if it does happen, they're ready for it. It doesn't hurt to explain beforehand how you'd like them to react, if the worst does happen. It may feel like you're almost preparing for a war or something, but chances are nothing will happen and you'll have a nice walk. All you're actually doing is preparing in case things do go badly.

- If you can't face going out, then consider a virtual walk. Sometimes I just can't manage to go outside, even though I know it might help. When I feel like this, I take a visit to my virtual walking playlist. This is a list of videos, webcams and nature sounds that help me feel calm and relaxed. Things on my list include a video of someone walking through a Scandinavian forest, someone gently skiing down a mountain, webcams set up in various national parks across the globe, and soothing bird songs. We are surrounded by all this technology nowadays and we can make it work for us in amazing ways, especially when it comes to anxiety. If you can't go to the mountain, then get the mountain to come to you. It's the future and we can do this stuff now!

Cry

Crying, for some of us, is a difficult thing to do. It's a very raw response to strong emotions and can open up doors you might not want open. The thing is, though, it can be good for us.

I sometimes joke that it hasn't been a successful therapy session if I haven't cried at some point during those 50 minutes; but, like the best jokes, there's actually a lot of truth in that as well. For instance, I know that when I cry because of something I'm feeling, it's something important that I should explore further.

I also know that in the moments where I've let it out and properly cried, I've felt better afterwards. Science, it seems, is undecided about why we even cry at all, but to me it feels like a way of letting out emotion or tension that is otherwise unbearable, which can only ever help when it comes to anxiety.

Things that cost money

Sometimes we have to spend a little to get something. Sometimes we wish that this wasn't the case; but, actually, by spending money on something you hope will help with your anxiety, you're also investing in yourself. Some of the following ideas will be more expensive than others, but where that is the case, I'll try to indicate that in the text.

Pets!

Pets can be great for anxiety. They feel nice to touch, and they offer companionship, love and purpose to our lives. We've been using them to help with our wellbeing for centuries.

There have been countless studies on the mental health benefits of having animals in your life, and they can offer a lot for anyone experiencing anxiety.

Obviously, having a pet is a commitment. It can also be expensive, depending on what kind of animal you choose to live with you. It's not an undertaking to be taken lightly, but it can be very fulfilling – certainly in my own experience, it's incredibly positive and life-boosting.

Check out your local animal shelter/rescue centre for more information!

Music

Music is amazing. There's something magical and unique about it, and it can really help with our anxiety. Creating an anxiety playlist can be an extremely useful tool to help tackle our anxiety, and it's very easy to do.

Start with songs you know, and work from there. Think about how the music makes you feel, and also how you'd like to feel. A lot of music platforms have smart algorithms nowadays, so they can even start recommending things they think you might like, based on what you're listening to. In addition, you can often do searches using keywords like 'calm', or 'soothing'. If you're struggling to get started, it's worth checking out other people's playlists – there are loads out there on the internet you can use as a starting point.

It's worth considering all types of music – lyrical, instrumental, classical, pop, whatever really – the key is finding the tunes that create the feeling you're looking for inside of you.

So how does music help with anxiety? Music affects our brain. Sad songs that resonate with us stimulate the same part of our brain that controls things like crying, and happy songs can create euphoric feelings. Some of us are even lucky enough to get the chills (science calls this the 'pilomotor reflex'), like goose bumps, when we hear music that deeply resonates with us. Music is powerful and magical. It feeds our hearts and our souls, and it can really help with our anxiety. The complexities of music – the pitch, the tone, the dynamics – all stimulate our brain in a myriad of different ways and can lift us out of depressive and challenging times.

Research (by Dr David Lewis-Hodgson of Mindlab International) suggests that the right music can reduce anxiety by 65 per cent.[2] The researchers even created a tune to do exactly this (it's by Marconi Union, and it's called 'Weightless', if you want to check it out).[3]

Music has been a powerful tool for my own anxiety, and I have so many memories of times where it has lifted away all my troubles. I remember being at the front of a gig by a band called The Walkmen, when they performed a song called 'The Rat'. Often I find gigs a strange combo of exciting and anxiety-inducing, but

---

2   Mindlab (2019) 'A Study Investigating the Relaxation Effects of the Music Track *Weightless* by Marconi Union in Consultation with Lyz Cooper.' Available at www.britishacademyofsoundtherapy.com/wp-content/uploads/2019/10/Mindlab-Report-Weightless-Radox-Spa.pdf.

3   Curtin, C. (2017) 'Neuroscience says listening to this song reduces anxiety by up to 65 per cent.' Available at www.inc.com/melanie-curtin/neuroscience-says-listening-to-this-one-song-reduces-anxiety-by-up-to-65-per cent.html.

in the moment when the music started I felt something change. As the song built to its climax, the euphoria and feeling of peace I felt was remarkable. Another time, I remember seeing Emmy the Great at a local venue. Halfway through the gig she turned on the lights and handed out lyric sheets to Leonard Cohen's song 'Anthem'. She asked everyone to sing along with her as she performed a cover of the song, as an act of solidarity and connection in a sometimes troubling and dark world. It was honestly one of the most beautiful and amazing things I've ever experienced. Everyone sang their hearts out, and for a moment it was like we were all connected. It was a powerful moment and it's a memory that I still fall back on in times of trouble. (I still have the song sheet, in a little frame – it was that special.)

Music is powerful and remarkable, and it can really help with anxiety.

Gardening/window boxes/houseplants

Growing things can be incredibly calming. I have an allotment, and it's one of my go-to places when I'm feeling anxious, in part because it has become a sanctuary, away from the hustle and bustle of the city, but also because there's something meditative about nurturing plants.

If you're not lucky enough to have a garden or an allotment, then even something as simple as a window box or some house-plants can help. You can grow herbs or salad vegetables quite easily in a window box, and then as a plus you get tasty snacks as well.

If you don't have space for a window box, then houseplants can be soothing as well, and kinda quite addictive once you get into them! Easy houseplants to care for include spider plants, succulents, *Dracaena*, *Monstera* ('Swiss cheese plant' as it's more commonly known) and *Philodendron*.

Plants are great for wellbeing generally, and anxiety especially. They do cool stuff like help purify the air around you; and some of them, like lavender, have calming scents that help with sleep anxiety and help take our minds off of the things that trouble us.

Tending to plants can be calming and restorative, and various scientific studies across the globe have confirmed this.[4]

As a bonus, plants can be beautiful as well. As humans we love to be near things we find aesthetically pleasing. They make us happy and calm, and plants massively fit this bill.

Baking

Let's talk baking, and in particular bread making. One of the best things I've learnt to do is bake. And you know why it's one of the best things? Because it really helps with my anxiety.

There is something so magical about baking bread. It's remarkably simple at its core, but you can make it much more complex if you wish. It has a very clear and simple method, it doesn't cost much to do, and you get something amazing at the end.

Baking helps you relax because it's so focused. You get to use your hands, and in the case of bread making you get to really work the dough, squashing, pulling, kneading all those fears, worries and frustrations out.

It can be very nurturing as well, as you can bake for other

---

4   Van Den Berg, A.E. and Custers, M.H.G. (2010) 'Gardening promotes neuro-endocrine and affective restoration from stress.' Available at https://journals.sagepub.com/doi/abs/10.1177/1359105310365577; Kuo, F.E. (Ming) (2010) *Parks and Other Green Environments: Essential Components of a Healthy Human Habitat.* Available at www.nrpa.org/uploadedFiles/nrpa.org/Publications_and_Research/Research/Papers/MingKuo-Research-Paper.pdf; Lee, M., Lee, J., Park, B-J. and Miyazaki, Y. (2015) 'Interaction with indoor plants may reduce psychological and physiological stress by suppressing autonomic nervous system activity in young adults: a randomized crossover study.' Available at www.ncbi.nlm.nih.gov/pmc/articles/PMC4419447.

people, be they friends, neighbours or family. Sharing something you've made – something that literally sustains people's lives – feels like an amazing and powerful thing to do and can really help with feelings of belonging and connection.

When I'm making bread it's almost like meditation in that it puts me into this calm place with the repetition of kneading the dough and the structure of the recipe. It's easy to lose yourself in the process, which in the case of anxiety reduction is a very good thing. At the back of this book there's a bread recipe you can try out, but there are loads of books, websites and videos out there as well with info on how to bake.

If baking isn't your thing, there are plenty of other options as well. People have reported feeling reduction in anxiety levels from making jam, learning to cook new things, wine making, home brewing, knitting and so much more.

Therapy

If you can find the right therapist, then this can work wonders. The downsides are that it takes time (like potentially years) to work, it costs money, and it's at its most effective if you do it regularly (like weekly), which means it can really add up cost-wise.

The big upside, though, is that exploring what makes you tick with someone else can be very helpful, and sometimes life-changing.

It's not unusual to find therapy very challenging, especially at the start. It can be surreal and awkward trying to share how you feel with someone who is essentially a complete stranger. I found that at the start it helped me to remember that I had control in this situation about how much I gave. It was also helpful for me to remember that at the simplest level I was paying someone to listen to me talk, so I should probably try and get my money's worth.

Make sure you find a therapist that works for you and understands what you want from them. It's not therapy if you spend the entire time explaining what trans or non-binary means, so having someone that already understands this stuff can help as well.

I make a point of never lying in therapy. It makes it tough sometimes, but it's also liberating having a space where you only ever say exactly how you feel, without having to sugar-coat it or change what you mean so as to make it more palatable for others.

There are many options when it comes to therapy, so if you're considering it, it's worth doing some research beforehand to explore what might be best for you. Below are some of the main types you'll come across:

- *Cognitive behavioural therapy (CBT):* This is perhaps one of the more well-known types of therapy, especially when it comes to anxiety. It's very effective for a lot of people and is widely used. CBT, at its simplest, is all about identifying negative thoughts and patterns, and then replacing them with more realistic and helpful ones, using various actions and coping mechanisms. It can take a while to achieve your goals within CBT, as you're effectively re-training how your brain thinks, so it's often best approached as a long-term commitment.

- *Exposure therapy:* This is a form of CBT and can help you tackle anxieties and fears more directly. Over time, your therapist will gradually expose you to the things that cause you anxiety, using a technique called systematic desensitization. This can be done through your imagination, real life or even virtual reality. This obviously can be quite full-on, but exposure therapy can give you some effective tools in dealing with specific fears and anxieties.

- *Dialectical behaviour therapy (DBT):* This is another form of CBT and is used to help change unhelpful behaviours you might have. It often has a stronger focus on accepting who you are, using the relationship between yourself and your therapist as a catalyst for change.

- *Art therapy:* This is often nonverbal and uses art and creativity to explore emotions and feelings. It's sometimes used in conjunction with other types of therapy.

- *Psychoanalytic therapy:* This is your classic Freudian therapy and can be quite intensive as you explore your thoughts, fears and desires.

- *Interpersonal therapy:* This includes exploring your relationships with others and any issues around that. Again, this can be quite intense and might mean going to some difficult places in terms of relationships with others.

- *Holistic therapy:* This can include things like acupuncture, massage, yoga, tai chi and reiki. Again, these things are often used in conjunction with other therapies.

- *Life coaching:* A life coach is someone who, rather than giving you specific advice or counselling, will help you achieve specific goals in life. They'll look at where you are now, and what's limiting where you want to be, and then help you change this. I've included life coaching as a potential option because a lot of people find this approach very helpful. A good life coach can be like a personal trainer for your anxiety battles, helping you stay on track with support and encouragement. Life coaching can help you especially with things like resilience building and motivation.

- *Shaking therapy, or trauma release exercises (TRE):* This is based on the idea that when animals experience trauma and shock, they start shaking, often quite violently, to enable themselves to recover. The shaking is believed to help release tension, stress and anxiety within our bodies. The technique has gained a lot of popularity over the last few decades, and although I've never tried it, I know others that have found it extremely helpful and continue to use the techniques they've learnt as ongoing self-care.

The key, as with so much when it comes to anxiety, is finding out what works for you. Therapy only works well if it's something that you actively want to do, so explore your options, and don't be afraid to change therapies, or therapists, if they're not proving the right choice for you or where you are in your life.

Long-term things

These things might be a bit more time-consuming or challenging, so you might need to put aside some time for them. They might not get you instant results but they are worth persevering with!

Find out what you're sensitive to

We can be sensitive to many things, both emotionally and in terms of what we eat. The way things affect us, and how we feel and react, can trigger anxiety. If we can work out what stuff causes a reaction, then we can try and avoid it and hopefully lessen the times we get anxious!

Food sensitivities are something we can get tested for, but we don't always need to because there are some things that are common culprits. Food and drinks that can potentially increase anxiety include:

- anything with caffeine in it (so coffee, energy drinks)
- food with a high sugar content (basically sweets, cakes and chocolate, some fruit juices)
- processed foods (ready meals, white bread)
- alcohol
- high-fat foods.

Annoyingly, all these foods are pretty tasty, and sort of addictive. We know that sugars, for instance, are a quick and easy fix of energy for our bodies. In terms of survival, it makes sense for us to consume sugar if we find it, because it'll give us the immediate energy we need to find more food sources. Nowadays, we live in a world where sugar, fat and salt are all readily available to a lot of us, but the need to consume them hasn't caught up with this.

There are, however, foods out there that can potentially help with managing anxiety. A lot of these are kind of obvious, but it's worth repeating them here:

- *Citrus fruit* (oranges, lemons, fruit high in vitamin C).
- *Green vegetables* (broccoli, kale, rocket, chard, asparagus, avocados).
- *Magnesium.* Studies have shown a potential improvement in anxiety symptoms in people who had magnesium in their diet. Sources of magnesium include green leafy vegetables, almonds, oats, sunflower seeds and sesame seeds.

- *Camomile tea*. It's a real classic, and one of those things that's often suggested as a calming drink before sleeping.

- *Dark chocolate*. Hold on. Didn't you just say chocolate is bad? Well, yes, but actually, like so many things, it's not that simple. Dark chocolate (anything 70% cocoa or higher) actually can potentially help reduce stress. Dark chocolate has a lot of antioxidants in it, which can help lower blood pressure, which in turn can help stress and anxiety. Just avoid eating any before bed, as it can also make you more alert, and wake you up.

- *Fish*. There's increasingly more and more evidence that omega-3 fatty acids, found in fish such as salmon, tuna, sardines, trout and mackerel, are really great for making you feel uplifted and in a better mood. They are also high in protein, which is another thing that can increase mental energy and alertness. Other protein sources include eggs, cheese, nuts and beans.

- *Whole grains*, so things like brown bread, whole-wheat pasta, and brown rice. These all contain carbohydrates, which help produce serotonin in our brains. We sometimes refer to serotonin as one of the happiness hormones, along with endorphins and dopamine. It also has been linked to better sleep patterns, which can only be a good thing.

- *Water*. This is more about drinking enough water. Dehydration will make you feel terrible, no question, and most of us don't drink enough water every day. Recommended amounts do vary, but the most important thing is to just remember to drink some water. Not drinking enough can make you tired, affect your skin's health and harm your body. These things can lead to anxiety because you feel like crap.

With all of this, it's worth pointing out that you don't have to suddenly stop eating sweets or drinking coffee. In reality, it's not that easy to stop eating the things we like. A lot of things like chocolate and junk food actually make us feel better for a short while, even if long term they're not great for us. As I write this, I've just eaten two chocolate bars, so I can't really talk.

Maybe the best way to look at it is this. You now have some information about food and how it affects anxiety. It's a jumping-on point if you want to research it some more, but it's also information you now have that you can maybe do something with, if you want to. It doesn't have to mean a huge shift; it could just mean you eat a portion of broccoli a couple of times a week, or eat an orange rather than buy some orange squash.

Keep a diary
Writing things down can be hugely helpful. I've kept diaries on and off for years, and sometimes it's very useful to be able to look back through them and see how you were a year ago. This can help with perspective as well.

Diaries don't need to be elaborate or complex. You can write about everything you've done that day, or you can just write bullet points. You can draw or write. You can even invent your own secret language and write using that.

The trick with diaries is to be honest in them. Your diary should be a private thing for your thoughts and feelings, and you shouldn't share it. Writing down your anxieties can often help your brain to process them, and it can help with working out issues and difficulties as you're getting stuff out of your head. By putting all the worries onto the page, you're making space in your head to start working out what's going on. Of course, this is most effective if you're also being truthful, which is why it's important to keep it private. What you write will inevitably change if you know someone else will read it. (You can try it as an exercise for your diary: write about your day as if you were telling your parents or partner, and then do the same thing just for you.)

If a full-on diary feels like too much, then you could also try bullet journalling – it's like a 21st-century diary, where you use a grid to write stuff down and draw things. You can make lists, keep a diary, and make it look nice with illustrations. The creativity you can put into your journal can also really help with anxiety.

Sleep better

Sleeping is, for a lot of us, a bit of a thing. It's absolutely essential for us to be able to survive, but it's also something that can elude us, especially when it comes to anxiety. It's rough as well because if you don't get quality sleep it just makes anxiety worse, in part because you're tired and in part because you start to get anxiety around sleeping, and the lack of it. All you want to do is just switch off and go to sleep, but it can feel like your brain is actively working against you when insomnia strikes.

Sorting this out can feel almost impossible, but there are things you can do.

- Cognitive behavioural therapy (CBT) is something a lot of people turn to when it comes to sleep disorders. We've mentioned CBT before, and it's a therapy that's used a lot when it comes to anxiety. The thinking with CBT is that by challenging negative thoughts and replacing them with realistic thoughts, you'll start to change how you think, and the way that you feel.

    A classic example in relation to sleep would be thinking, 'Why can't I sleep like a normal person? Everyone else can do it so why can't I?'

A realistic counter to this would be 'Loads and loads of people struggle with sleep, including other people I know. It's not just me, and I know that I can get better at it with time and practice.'

CBT is something that you normally have to pay for, because to get the most benefit you need a trained CBT therapist to guide you. CBT can take a while to start working and is not a cure, but it can be really effective in providing tools to help you manage your anxiety and sleep issues.

- Cut down on caffeine-based food and drinks a few hours before you go to bed. Sounds obvious, but it's worth repeating.

- Make your bedroom a peaceful place, like a sanctuary. You can do this with soft lighting, quietness and temperature. We sleep better in rooms that are peaceful and cool (in a temperature-type way – the jury's still out on whether a cool as in awesome room helps with sleep).

- Sometimes if I'm struggling with sleep, I watch TV. My go-to programme is *Grand Designs* because it's easy to watch. It follows a pretty strict formula (people want to build a house, they run out of money because it costs way more than they thought, Kevin is doubtful it's all going to come together in time, it all comes together in time, there's a nice house to look at) and it's light enough to distract me, without also involving me too much. Basically, it's soothing to a noisy brain.

Interestingly, I know quite a few people who do this to help with sleep, although everyone's 'sleep programme' is different. I've heard people say they use *Friends* (the US comedy), *Tiny House Nation* (another house-building programme), *The Simpsons* or any other number of telly shows. I also know quite a few people who listen to podcasts as a way of getting to sleep.

· Medication is also an option. These can be prescribed by your GP and can help if things are proving too much. Some sleeping pills are addictive, though, so are not considered a long-term solution. Alternative options such as acupuncture, meditation and herbal remedies (for example, valerian root, chamomile and lemon balm) have all been used for treating sleep disorders. It's important to check with your doctor first if you're considering alternative medication, as some have side effects, can interact with other medication you might be taking or shouldn't be taken if you're pregnant.

· Do calming things before you go to bed. Getting yourself into a tranquil place before sleep can help a lot. Keep your mood chilled and quiet by maybe reading a book or having a bath.

· Weighted blankets can help generally with anxiety but they can also help with sleep. The thinking behind them is that the weight calms us by grounding us, simulating deep-pressure touch and encouraging our brains to release various hormones including serotonin and melatonin. Some people find these blankets amazing, whilst others are a bit meh, so it's a try-it-and-see type of thing.

Unfortunately, the thing with sleeping better is that it isn't going to happen overnight, if you'll excuse the pun. It will take time and practice, but it can really help with any anxiety you feel. Honestly, once you get a good night's sleep, you'll wake up feeling so much better and refreshed, and ultimately less anxious.

Exercise

Exercise is something that can help a lot with anxiety, but it's also something that works best when it's done regularly.

There are lots of different ways to exercise, but I know when I think about exercise my mind just jumps to all the times I've tried to do exercise and failed. I can't even count how many times I've joined a gym, gone once and then never gone again. (Okay, it's 12 times. I *can* count the times; it's just I'd rather not). Our anxious brains, of course, love to fixate on the failures, rather than, for instance, the time I did join a gym and went regularly for over a year.

For me, it's easy to want to start exercising. I know it helps with my anxiety and makes me feel good about my body and how I look. Being stronger and fitter makes me feel safer as well, which in turn helps with other anxieties I often feel, so I very much want to start doing it. The hard bit for me – and I suspect for a lot of others – is sticking with it. The important thing is to find a form of exercise that you enjoy. There's no point jogging round the block 20 times if you hate running.

Joining a gym is potentially quite scary. They can feel super-intimidating and very overwhelming. If you're considering this option, then doing some research is a good idea. To help with this, here are some ideas based on my own experiences:

- Find out if any of your trans friends go to a gym, and if so which one. It's also worth checking out websites for reviews and seeing if the gym has an inclusion policy.

- If you're feeling brave, ask the gym you're thinking of joining what they do to ensure the safety and respect of their trans clients. Finding out what their policies are towards trans people can be really helpful.

- Find out if the gym has unisex, communal or gendered changing rooms and toilets. I used to get changed before I went to the gym because I felt more comfortable doing that, but it's good to get all the info you need so you can make an informed decision.

- Exercise with a friend. I found that I was more likely to exercise if I had someone with me. Again, there's safety in numbers, but also having a pal along with me was encouraging, and we could mutually support each other to get fit.

Medication

There are various anti-anxiety medications out there you can take. The main ones tend to be things like antidepressants, beta blockers, benzodiazepines and buspirone. They work in a variety of different ways: some affect our blood pressure and heart rate, such as beta blockers, and aren't considered so great long term; others, such as antidepressants, help our brain make serotonin and are considered more of a longer-term solution. As always, these medications can have side effects, and can be addictive, so are something that should only be prescribed by a qualified medical professional.

A lot of people find medication incredibly helpful, and I know for me it was vital. It helped me get a head start on my anxiety and depression, and cleared my mind enough to be able to then start practising methods of self-care.

There are a lot of different ways to help yourself when it

comes to anxiety. I've spoken about the things that have worked well for me, but there will no doubt be countless other ways as well that I haven't mentioned. As I've said before, you need to find what works for you, and then do it.

There are a couple of other more general things that are also important when it comes to self-care and anxiety, so let's take a quick look at them before we wrap up this chapter.

Recognize (and celebrate) your achievements

It is vital that you recognize that you're doing something about your anxiety and know how important that is. Just by reading this book you're doing something, and it's good to celebrate that. Reward yourself for doing something to help your anxiety. Some people may well say that doing the thing should be its own reward, and, yeah, it can be, but also you really should reward yourself for doing something.

The things you try to do to help yourself are hard to do, dealing with anxiety is hard to do, so recognize and celebrate this. It could just be some self-affirmation and praise, or having a nice meal, or going to the cinema, or playing a game for an hour. Give yourself a break, cut yourself some slack, and know you did a good thing.

Practise self-care on your terms

Self-care is quite the thing at the moment. It's all over social media, hashtagged, commercialized and packaged up in little neat boxes. It's also all so perfect. With this perfection, of course, comes another thing: pressure.

It can feel like there's a correct way to practise self-care, like you have to reach these goals, tick these boxes, and be this positive, motivated amazing person in order to do it right. Just by searching #selfcare, #wellbeing or #selflove, for example, you'll be bombarded by the many, many 'right' ways to do it, and it's all quite intense, and anxiety-inducing. It can be a bit much sometimes, and I think it's pretty clear that if your self-care is making you anxious, then it's not actually self-care.

Self-care has become a product and a currency in our world, and that's not always helpful, because with that we're also sold a big lie: that there's a correct way to practise all this and manage our anxiety and tackle our stress.

It's very important to remember that there is no right way. There's only your way. Find out what works for you and do that.

CHAPTER 11

Endings, Beginnings and How to Make It Better

At the beginning of this book I asked the question 'Do I want to feel like this?' It feels like a simple question, with a simple answer; but, of course, anxiety is never simple. Anxiety is complex, messy and difficult.

We've spoken a lot about ways to tackle anxiety, and I hope that something you've read in this book has helped, even if just a little. Sometimes all we need is an edge, a tiny, slight advantage to get us ahead enough to change things up, especially when it feels like so much is stacked against us.

I think one of the most important things I've learnt about anxiety, about my anxiety, is that getting better from anxiety doesn't mean it goes away. All those feelings, all those strong, emotional, scary feelings, don't suddenly disappear or feel less full-on. The anxiety doesn't always becomes less intense or less frequent. The things that cause you anxiety don't go away.

I still feel it all sometimes, and, yeah, sometimes it still feels like too much.

When I first started exploring my anxiety, I had this end

goal of eliminating it, of reaching this place where I was all carefree and just always okay. Of course, it didn't take me long to realize that approaching anxiety with the goal of eliminating it is a lost cause, because anxiety is a part of life. The trick with getting better from anxiety is becoming better at managing it, and recognizing it for what it is: a natural, normal part of being alive and being human.

Anxiety can often feel like this monster inside us. It can feel wrong and dark and oppressive. It can feel out of control and out of proportion, and for me a big part of managing this was recognizing that, and then trying to see past it.

It's not easy – I think we can all agree on that point – and we're all going to deal with anxiety differently, because we are all different.

My ways might not work for you, so the trick is finding the ways that work for who you are. You need to find your thing, using the clues you gather along the way.

It's good to not be lured in by the magical cure-all solution, even though it would be so much easier if there was such a thing. There is no one way out, but rather a whole toolbox of answers, each tuned for a different situation.

Anxiety is such a fluid thing. You'll feel better one day and less so another, and it can strike in so many ways, from so many different angles, so it's good to have a variety of solutions for when it does. What works in your own home, for instance, might not be ideal when you're out and about, and vice versa.

Once you have a variety of different ways to tackle your anxiety, you'll be on fire, and those bad days will become easier to manage. And the beauty of it all is that the more you use these anxiety-busting skills, the more effective they'll become.

You're taking back the power you have always had inside you, one step at a time.

Anxiety is rooted in feeling powerless, in being disempowered. Getting that power back can change a lot.

It's easy to just give up, to feel that none of this is worth it, and that your anxiety is just too much to bear. The world is full of things that tell us we're not worth it, that we're right to be afraid, to be anxious. There's always something else ready to bring us down. As I write this, in 2020, the world feels like a very unsafe place to be for us as trans people. In the USA, the government has been systematically stripping away rights for marginalized groups, with a particular focus on trans people. Across the rest of the world, we hear about countries declaring themselves LGBTQ+-free zones, about the death squads and LGBTQ+ purges. As trans people, we're often at the forefront of all this hate, because of our visibility, because our media demonizes and scapegoats us, and because a lot of the people in positions of power and influence right now are transphobic, homophobic, racist and misogynistic.

It's absolutely heart-breaking.

It's so short-sighted, prejudiced and cruel as well, especially as some of it comes from people that should be our allies.

It makes you – no, it makes me – just want to give up.

It makes me want to cut myself off, retreat and hide away, and never do anything ever again.

It makes me afraid, and that's an awful thing to feel.

Here's where it gets extremely hard as well, because now I have to make a choice none of us should ever have to make.

Do I just give up?

I feel powerless, I feel anxious, and I feel alone. Giving up feels like just one step away.

Here's the thing, though. All of us out there with anxiety, with depression, with loss, and fear and pain, we all have one thing in common:

We feel things.

We really feel things. That's why all this shit affects us so much. That's why we feel afraid, or sad, or in pain. We are the empaths.

I know it's almost a trope by now but I do believe that we, as trans people, are special with our 'empathicness' and our ability to feel. Our anxiety is also a strength. It's a super-power.

I know it doesn't always feel that way – hells do I know. Our anxiety is a symptom of our power to feel. We easily get overwhelmed by it, because it's so strong, and so intense, but it's telling us something important.

It's telling us that something needs to change, and we might just be the only people that can make it happen.

We have a choice. We can give in to it all, we can hide away, and we can call it quits. Or we can fight.

We can push back. We cannot disappear like the haters want us to. We can stay visible. We can shout about who we are and why we're here.

We can support each other through the tough times, we can stop looking inwards and getting caught up in the web of what counts as trans enough to be trans, and just accept that we are all in this together. Collectively we are the force for change. That's why they push so hard against us. That's why they want us to feel anxious and depressed. They think that if they hurt us enough, we'll just go away, that we'll shut up, and that they'll win this strange and ill-informed war they think they're fighting.

It's tough, I know – the things worth fighting for often are – but it's also worth it.

Overcoming anxiety is the ultimate act of empowerment. It's about investing and believing in yourself. By tackling your anxiety head-on, and trying your best to manage it, to not let it get you down, you're also saying, 'I'm worth this. I am worth something; I am worth everything.'

Anxiety often feels like it's all about other people and how they affect you, which can leave you feeling pretty powerless.

If you feel like you can't do it any more, like it's all just too much, then just stop. Take a moment to catch your breath and think about what you can do to empower yourself. Think about what you can do right now to make this situation better.

Sometimes you're actually the only one with the power to do something, so try to be kind to yourself. When you can, help others, but remember that you can only do this if you also help yourself.

Listen to what your mind and your body are telling you. Take a break and catch your breath when you can, and definitely when you need to.

Find an outlet for all your pain. Maybe it's writing, singing or poetry – it doesn't matter what as long as it works for you. Make it first and foremost for you, do what you do like nobody's watching, make it personal, make it private, do it for you and you alone.

I hope that within this book there's something that helps, and I hope that you come away with some extra tools for your anxiety toolkit. I hope, as well, that you're doing okay, and that if you're not, that there's an end in sight somewhere for you, even if it seems far away right now.

I'm going to finish up with something I wrote before I'd even thought about writing a book about anxiety, because it's something I need to remember, and it's something that anxiety tries to make me forget.

Sometimes it blows my mind that I've been able to do the things I've done, that I'm able to have the things I didn't think I could have.

I look back and think if only past me knew, if only she knew where we would be today, right now.

She would be so proud, so impressed, and so amazed that we'd come so far in such a short time. 'Look what we did,' I'd say.

Look how amazing we are.

The Anxiety Toolkit

Something I've found useful in dealing with my anxiety is the series of questions below. I call it my anxiety toolkit and I'm sharing it with you now, in case it's useful. It basically breaks down anxiety into manageable chunks that I can then process more easily, which then enables me to develop better coping strategies when anxiety hits. The questions give me a way of recording facts about my anxiety, and also then give me a reference point for later on, which can be very helpful for future anxiety attacks as well.

- What are my triggers?

- What do I have control over, and what do I not?

- What signs/symptoms are there that I'm feeling anxious?

- What can I do now/in the moment to help?

- What can I do later?

- What should I remember for next time?

Further Reading and Resources

Books

Anxiety Is Really Strange by Steve Haines (Author) & Sophie Standing (Illustrator), Singing Dragon.

Before I Step Outside (You Love Me) by Travis Alabanza, self-published.

Cheer Up Love: Adventures in Depression with the Crab of Hate by Susan Calman, Two Roads.

Complex PTSD: From Surviving to Thriving – A Guide and Map for Recovering from Childhood Trauma by Pete Walker, self-published.

Gender Outlaws: The Next Generation by Kate Bornstein, Seal Press.

Good Food for Bad Days: What to Make When You're Feeling Blue by Jack Monroe, Bluebird.

Rewriting the Rules by Meg-John Barker, Routledge.

Sister Outsider by Audre Lorde, Penguin Classics.

The Body Keeps the Score: Mind, Brain and Body in the Transformation of Trauma by Dr Bessel van der Kolk, Penguin.

The Trans Partner Handbook by Jo Green, Jessica Kingsley Publishers.

The Trans Teen Survival Guide by Fox and Owl Fisher, Jessica Kingsley Publishers.

The Voice Book for Trans and Non-Binary People: A Practical Guide to Creating and Sustaining Authentic Voice and Communication by Matthew Mills and Gillie Stoneham, Jessica Kingsley Publishers.

Trans Power by Juno Roche, Jessica Kingsley Publishers.

Waking The Tiger: Healing Trauma – The Innate Capacity to Transform Overwhelming Experiences by Peter A. Levine, North Atlantic Books.

Your Resonant Self: Guided Meditations and Exercises to Engage Your Brain's Capacity for Healing by Sarah Peyton, W. W. Norton & Company.

Organizations and websites

Category Is Books – An independent LGBTQIA+ bookshop in the southside of Glasgow. It also offers groups and a social space.

www.categoryisbooks.com

Christella VoiceUp – An app (available for android and iPhone) that has voice training lessons to help feminise your voice. Features in-app purchases.

https://speechtools.co/christella-voiceup

Gendered Intelligence – A London-based youth organization, working with trans and gender exploring/questioning young people.

http://genderedintelligence.co.uk

Gender Stories – A podcast hosted by Alex Iantaffi, featuring guests from across the world, who discuss their gender identity, and how that affects their lives.

https://www.alexiantaffi.com/podcast

Mermaids – A UK charity that supports children and young people who are exploring their gender identity/gender-diverse, and their families.

https://mermaidsuk.org.uk

Helpline 0808 801 0400

Mindline Trans+ – A national helpline offering emotional support for trans people in the UK.

https://bristolmind.org.uk/help-and-counselling/ mindline-transplus

Helpline 0300 330 5468

Open Barbers – A London-based hairdressing service for all lengths, genders and sexualities. They offer a personalized and warm haircutting experience with a queer- and trans-friendly attitude.

https://openbarbers.com

Praat – An open-source program for the analysis of speech in phonetics, created by Paul Boersma and David Weenink of the University of Amsterdam.

www.praat.org

Reddit – Reddit is a social media website. It's made up of forums called subreddits, focused around particular subjects. These are some of the subreddits I've found useful:

r/transvoice
r/asktransgender
r/transhealth
r/Anxiety
r/Anxietyhelp
r/Transgender_Surgeries

http://reddit.com

Refuge Restrooms – Safe places to pee for trans and non-binary people.

www.refugerestrooms.org

Top Trans-Inclusive Employers – Stonewall's list of trans-inclusive employers.

www.stonewall.org.uk/top-trans-inclusive-employers

Trans Can Sport – A not-for-profit project based in Brighton & Hove. It was created to get trans people into exercise and healthy living and aims to help anyone who feels their transgender identity makes participating in sport difficult, including people who are questioning or exploring their gender.

www.transcansport.co.uk

Trans Lifeline – Trans-led national helpline in the USA and Canada.

www.translifeline.org

Bread for Anxious People

You're going to need...

500g strong white flour (You can also use strong brown flour if you want, but the key thing is that you get strong flour as it's made specially for bread making. You can get it in pretty much any supermarket.)

2 teaspoons of salt

2 teaspoons of sugar

7g sachet of dried yeast (Sometimes this is called fast-acting yeast. It's basically yeast that's all ready to get going – no need to activate it, this yeast just wants to raise your bread stat!)

3 tablespoons of olive oil

300ml of warm water (You might not need all of this, and it needs to be warm – like you can easily put your fingers in it and it's just quite pleasantly warm.)

This is what you do...

1. Get a bowl and put the flour, salt, sugar and yeast in it. Mix those bad boys up with your paws or a wooden spoon. It's all good. (When you add the yeast and the salt, make sure to put them on opposite sides of the bowl at first. This is because salt can kill yeast if it has too much direct contact, which isn't good.)

2. Make a well in the centre of the flour mixture, so it looks a bit like a crater. Pour the olive oil and about a third of the water into the well/crater and start mixing it up. Again, you can use a wooden spoon, but paws are way better. Get those hands in and start scrunching. Oh, also, make sure your hands are clean, otherwise you run the risk of making grey bread, which is basically bread with all the gross stuff on your hands mixed into it. No one wants that.

3. Keep adding more water and mixing it up until your dough looks not too dry and not too wet. If it's really sticky and claggy, add a tiny bit more flour. If it's all flaky and not holding together (relatable, I know), add a little bit more water. Eventually, you'll hit a sweet spot in the middle, which is where we get to the best bit.

4. Lightly flour a flat surface, like a table or kitchen counter. You don't need much flour – just enough to help stop the bread from sticking to the surface.

5. Now get your lump of dough and pop it on your floured surface and start kneading that beauty.

6. Never kneaded before? Don't worry, it's easy! The simplest

method to knead your amazing bread dough is to just fold the dough in half and squish forward on the heels of your hands to press it flat. Turn the dough slightly, fold it in half, and squish into it again with the heels of your hands. Just keep on doing that and you're good to go! However, if you want to be a bit more adventurous, you can also start stretching the dough outwards towards you, folding it back on itself and repeating that, or you can do a combo of both these methods, or make up your own! The idea with kneading is that you're making gluten, which forms when you move the dough around. The more you stretch, and squish, and generally pound the dough, the better. This is the best bit because it's really satisfying. All those troubles, worries, anxieties? Just let the dough take them. Squash them in, let the gluten take them, just be at one with the dough, even if it's just for a while.

7. Normally you need to knead for about 10 minutes, give or take. The dough should look all smooth and almost satin-like by now, so just put it back in the bowl you started mixing it in originally, and let it rest for a bit somewhere warm. You can put it next to a radiator, or in the airing cupboard if you have one, and cover the bowl with a tea towel to help with the rising.

8. Oh, yeah, the bread is going to rise. This bit is pretty joyful. You just leave it for 30 minutes to an hour, and when you come back, the dough should be loads bigger. This is because of our old pal the yeast!

9. This next bit seems a bit counter-intuitive, but trust me, you've got to do it. Get that lovely risen dough and knock the air out of it. That's right, squash it down! As

you squash it, you should be able to feel the air escape, which can feel kind of satisfying and cool.

10. Don't be too harsh with your squishing, I sometimes count the kneads I do, up to 30-ish, to make sure I don't overdo it.

11. Now you gently shape the dough! You could make a long loaf, or split it into three strands and plait it. You could make some little rolls, or pop it into a lightly oiled bread tin and let that shape your loaf. It's entirely up to you!

12. Once you've shaped your bread, then you need to let it rise again. Cover it with a tea towel, put it in a warm place and leave it for 30 minutes to an hour. It should start rising again pretty quickly.

13. Pop it in the oven at 200/220°C (fan/conventional oven temps) or gas mark 7, and bake for 15 to 30 minutes. You'll know it's ready, because when you tap the bottom, it'll sound hollow! Amazing!

14. Cool that loaf and then eat it all, knowing you made this! Once you've cracked bread making, you can make anything! I've made bagels, fruit loaves, ciabatta – the possibilities are endless.

Contributor Biographies

Meg-John Barker

Meg-John Barker is the author of a number of popular books on sex, gender and relationships, including *Queer: A Graphic History*, *Gender: A Graphic Guide*, *How To Understand Your Gender*, *Life Isn't Binary*, *Enjoy Sex (How, When, and IF You Want To)*, *Rewriting the Rules*, *The Psychology of Sex*, and *The Secrets of Enduring Love*. They have also written a number of books for scholars and counsellors on these topics, drawing on their own research and therapeutic practice.

Websites: rewriting-the-rules.com; megjohnandjustin.com

Twitter: @megjohnbarker | Instagram: @meg_john_barker

Sabah Choudrey

Reluctant activist on most things queer, brown and hairy. Proud trans youth worker since 2014. Public speaker, shy writer and psychotherapist in training. Interested in the fluidity of sexuality, gender and faith. Top three passions right now: carving out spaces for queer Muslims and trans people of colour, making friends with cats and taking selfies from bad angles.

Facebook: Sabah Choudrey | Twitter: @SabahChoudrey | Instagram: @sabah.c | sabahchoudrey.com

Maeve Devine

Maeve Devine is a musician, artist, writer and occasional hair stylist. A former support worker with a 16-year career, she specialized in supporting autistic adults and worked for eight years with the LGBTQ+ community both as a youth worker and a mental health advocate. She is fond of gentle people, dogs and cats, and she enjoys peace and quiet.

Effie

Effie (she/her) is a queer trans woman based in Brighton. Her music with The Effie Fowler Band explores identity, queerness, depression and anxiety. With two singles released to date ('Anxiety' and 'Coming Out'), you can keep up with the band at @effiefowlerband on Instagram and Facebook.

Rory Finn

Rory Finn lives in Brighton & Hove and has been trans and queer community-organizing for many years. He co-founded Trans Can Sport, and currently works in sexual health and writes for *Gscene* magazine. He is passionate about sex positivity and wellness. Can be found tweeting about such things @boyfinnbtn.

Roch

Roch lives at a number of intersections, and was diagnosed with ADHD, autism and dyspraxia in his early 30s (continuing to be in his early 30s at the time of writing). Having an understanding of his neurodivergence and how that interacts with his ethnicity, sexuality and transness has been pivotal in helping him address his experiences of anxiety, and he aims to use those experiences to support and mentor others who have gone through similar things.

Eris Young

Eris Young (they/them) is a queer, transgender writer of speculative fiction and nonfiction. Their first book, *They/Them/ Their: A Guide to Nonbinary and Genderqueer Identities*, came out from Jessica Kingsley Publishers in 2019. Their short fiction has appeared in magazines such as *Shoreline of Infinity* and *Astral Waters*, as well as anthologies such as *Uncanny Bodies*, published by Luna Press in August 2020. They were a recipient of a 2018 Queer Words Scotland Project mentorship, and are a recipient of a Scottish Book Trust New Writer Award for 2020. Find them on twitter @young_e_h.

Index

acceptance 37, 66–7, 138, 155–6, 181
accessing trans health care 133–41
achievements, recognizing and
    celebrating 191
affirmations *see* encouraging
    statements
alone time 169
alternative medication 188
American Psychiatric Association
    31
anger 58–63
anxiety
    as affecting people in different
        ways 9
    basics of 16–19
    celebrities with 13–14
    conclusions on 193–8
    denial of 15–16
    etymology of 12
    historical people with 15
    as important to survival 16
    managing 140–1
    nature of 11–12

notes on 24, 72–3, 115–16
and privilege and oppressions
    42–51
single sentence descriptions 24
and trans people 20–3
triggers 24, 123, 154, 182
voice 77–9
see also Freiya; myths
    about anxiety; personal
    experiences
anxiety disorders 19–20, 29, 110
anxiety toolkit 199
art therapy 181

Bachmann, C.L. 121
baking 178–9, 205–8
balanced thinking 62–3
Barker, M.-J. 141–4
Beckham, David 14
bedroom 187
Bell, Kristen 14
body dysmorphic disorder (BDD)
    89–91

bread making 205–8
breath control 27, 29, 170–2
breathing 28–9, 109, 115
bullet journalling 186

caffeine 183, 187
calming remedies 178, 184, 188
camomile tea 154, 184
Cannon, W.B. 16
celebrities with anxiety 13–14, 28
Center for American Progress 121
changing rooms 118–20, 190
chilling out 27
choice 80, 81, 83, 127, 196
Choudrey, S. 37–9
citrus fruit 183
cognitive behavioural therapy
    (CBT) 55, 180
    and sleep 186–7
colouring in 160
comfortable, feeling 109
coming out 35–6
    as anxiety-inducing 77, 118
    finding oneself 81–3
    opposition to 79–81
    personal experience of 75–7
    voice anxiety 77–9
communication (social media) 112
complex post-traumatic stress
    disorder (cPTSD) 142, 143–4
connection
    with others 167–8, 177
    with self 165
control
    and acceptance 67
    and anxiety 56
    over memories 170
    question related to 199
    and Stoicism 13, 30
    see also breath control

courage 116
Cox, Laverne 14
Crenshaw, K. 44
crossing bridges 166–7
crying 174
Curry, N.A. 160
Curtin, C. 176
Custers, M.H.G. 178

dance breaks 159
dark chocolate 184
Darwin, Charles 15
deferment 141
Devine, M. 128–31
dialectical behaviour therapy
    (DBT) 181
diaries 66, 108–9, 185–6
DiCaprio, Leonardo 14
Dickinson, Emily 15
distancing 54
distraction 139, 163
doing self down 127–8
doing something else 163
Du Bois, W.E.B. 43

Effie 153–6
'emotional flashback' 141–2, 143
encouraging statements 165–7
Equality Act (2010) 123
exercise 27, 37, 84–5, 189–90
exposure therapy 93–4, 180

555 technique 168
54321 technique 168–9
facial feminization surgery (FFS)
    33–4, 91–2, 135–6
fainting 28–9
fear 19, 67–71, 105–6
'feelings wheel' 57

fight or flight response 16–18, 142–3
finding oneself 81–3
see also identity
Finn, R. 83–5
fish 184
fluidity 100, 135
food sensitivities 182–5
Freiya
accessing trans health care 133–5, 136, 138–9
alone time 169
anger 58–62
anxiety 10–11, 17–18, 20–2, 24, 41–2, 72–3, 193–4
coming out 75–7, 80
crying 174
dating anxiety 124–6
exercise 189–90
fear 68–9
finding joy 145–8
finding self 80–1
gender dysphoria 87–9, 91–2, 93–4, 95–6, 158
job interviews and work 121–2
joy list 148–9
leaving (a situation) 164
music 176–7
privilege and oppressions 43, 44–5, 47–50
public toilets 151
relationships 127
sadness 64–7
'safe clothes' 172–3
sleep aid 187–8
social anxiety 60–1, 107
social media 110–12
sunlight 165
therapy 179–80
transitioning 117–18

friends
accompaniment on toilet visits 118
asking for support from 155
being truthful with 109–10
exercise with 190

gardening 177–8
gender dysphoria 90–3
definition 90
'dysphoria first-aid kit' 38
gender reassignment surgery 33–4
generalized anxiety disorder (GAD) 19
giving up 167, 195
goals 115
Gooch, B. 121
Grant, Hugh 14
gratitude journal 150–1
green vegetables 183
gyms 84–5, 189–90

herbs 27
Hippocrates 11–12
historical people with anxiety 15
holistic therapy 181
honesty 126–7, 185–6
hormone medication 36, 65, 91, 135, 138–9
houseplants 177–8
Human Rights Campaign 121
hyperventilation 28–9

Iantaffi, A. 144
identity
anxiety about 100, 102
fluid 100
gender 90

identity *cont.*
    other people questioning
        100–1
    see also finding oneself
innate fear 67
interpersonal therapy 181
'intersectionality' 44
introverts 28
invisibility 172–3

job interviews 28, 121–2
joy 145–8
    aids for finding 148–53
joy lists 148–9
judgement 97–8

Kardashian West, Kim 13
Kasser, T. 160
kindness
    to others 152
    to self 53, 124, 128
Kranz, G.S. 36
Kuo, F.E. (Ming) 178

Lady Gaga 14
learned fear 67–8, 69
leaving (a situation) 163–4, 166
Lee, M. 178
letting it all out 161
Lewis-Hodgson, D. 176
life coaching 181
Lincoln, Abraham 15

magnesium 183
mantras 165–7
Mao Zedong 166
McIntosh, P. 43
medical services, accessing 133–41

medication
    for anxiety 190–1
    hormone 36, 138–9
    myths relating to 25, 27, 36
    for sleep 188
    for social anxiety 110
    stigma around 55–6
meditation 170–2
melatonin 188
memories 170
mindfulness 27, 159–61
Mindlab International 176
Missy Elliot 13
money
    electrolysis vs therapy 157–8
    practical aids requiring 174–82
    saving 139
    for surgery 46, 96, 136
    ways of raising 48
    and work 121–4
Movement Advancement Project
    121
music 175–7
myths about anxiety 25–6, 36–7
    all trans people are anxious 34
    anxiety and happiness 32
    anxiety as cool 26
    anxiety as modern complaint
        26
    anxiety as not real/not an
        illness 29
    anxiety can be traced back to
        single bad experience 31–2
    anxiety medication interfering
        with hormone medication
        36
    breathing control 27
    coming out/fully transitioning
        will help with anxiety 35–6

cures for anxiety 27
forcing self is only way to
    overcome anxiety 30
gender reassignment surgery
    as cure for anxiety 33–4
general 25–33
as improving with time 27–8
only humans get anxiety 29
only some people get anxious
    26
only weirdos and freaks get
    anxious 28
panic attacks cause fainting
    28
people can snap out of anxiety
    30
people need to get over it, sort
    it out, stop whining 32–3
people with anxiety also suffer
    from other disorders 31
people with anxiety should
    avoid stressful situations
    29–30
professional help as con 30–1
stress and anxiety as same
    thing 28
successful people don't get
    anxiety 28
taking medication means
    being weak 25, 27
trans people as difficult due to
    anxiety 34–5
trans-specific 33–7
trans women as more anxious
    than trans men 35

National Center for Transgender
    Equality 121

National Health Service (NHS
    UK) 89–90, 136
nature 164–5, 174
Nicanor 11–12

oestrogen 36, 65
O'Keefe, Georgia 15
oppressions 42–5, 48–9, 51

panic attacks 28–9, 153, 165
panic disorder 19
'paper tiger' 166
perceived threat 17, 18, 59, 103
perfect day 149–50
permanence 127
personal experiences
    coming out 75–7
    Effie 153–6
    Eris 54–6
    feel and look of anxiety 54, 83,
        102, 128–9, 141–2, 153–4
    how being trans affects
        anxiety 39, 56, 85, 103–4,
        129–30, 155–6
    Maeve 128–31
    main aid for anxiety 56, 84–5,
        103, 155
    Meg-John 141–4
    Roch 97–102
    Rory 83–5
    Sabah 37–8
    single pieces of advice 38, 55–6,
        83, 103, 143–4, 154
    tips for feeling better 37–8, 54,
        83, 103, 115–16, 142–3, 154
    triggers 72–3
    see also Freiya
perspective, finding 116, 150–1
pets 29, 175

Peynton, S. 144
Phelps, Michael 14
phobia-based anxiety 19
planning
  for all outcomes 167
  for health care 137
  self-care 38
  for work 123
plants 177–8
podcasts 188
polarization 111
positivity 122
post-traumatic stress disorder
  (PTSD) 19, 31, 142, 143–4
practical aids 157–9
  costing money 174–82
  free 164–74
  long-term 182–92
  quick 159–64
Prince Harry 14
prioritizing tasks 37–8, 56
privilege 42–51
professional help myth 30–1
psychoanalytic therapy 181
public toilets 119, 120

reality checking 126, 161–2
Reisner, S.L. 36
relationships 35, 124–6, 181
research
  on anxiety disorders 29
  on music 176
  for work 122–3
resilience 51–3
resources 78
  books 201–2
  organizations and websites
    202–4
reward 85, 191
Reynolds, Ryan 14

Ritchie, H. 29
Roch 102–4
Roser, M. 29
Ross, B. 103
routines 170

sadness 63–7
'safe clothes' 172–3
saving 139
self-care
  on own terms 163, 191–2
  plans 38
  value of 154
self portrait photography 93–4
sensitivities 182–5
serotonin 36, 85, 152, 164, 184, 188,
  190
shaking therapy 182
sharing 34, 109–10, 113, 145, 179
'sisu' see resilience
sitting and waiting 139–40
sleep 186–9
social anxiety
  as common form of anxiety
    105
  definition 19
  help for 108–10
  personal experience of 60–1,
    107
  symptoms of 105–7
  and trans people 107–8
social media
  appropriate communication
    112
  different experiences of 112–13
  extremism on 108
  getting rid of 112
  limiting 111–12
  making it work 114
  as overwhelming 110–11

polarization 111
privacy 113
think before posting 113
trolls 113
spaces/services
    finding trans inclusive 120–1
    single-sex 118–20
speech therapy 77–8
spending time alone 169
starting small 94–5
Stewart, Kristen 13
Stoicism 12–13, 30
Stonewall 22, 121
street harassment 68–9
stress 28
stressful situations 29–30
stretching 163
sunsets and sunrises 164
surgery
    ability to afford scenario 46–51
    as gender dysphoria aid 95–7
    myth concerning 33–4
    as very expensive 136

talking
    to others 66, 70, 138–9
    to someone who 'gets' it 167–8
    to strangers, fear of 106
tea-making 161
TERF (trans-exclusionary radical
    feminist) 156
testosterone 36, 65, 77
therapy
    cost of 157–8
    myth concerning 30–1
    personal experience 41–2, 43
    as practical anxiety aid 179–80
    seeking 55–6
    types of 180–2

threat
    perceived 17, 18, 59, 103
    real 63, 107
time
    finding 158
    passing 139
    spending alone 169
transitioning
    as anxiety-inducing 117–18
    myth concerning 35–6
trans people
    accessing health care 133–41
    as agents of change 71
    and anxiety 20–3
    anxiety myths specific to 33–7
    finding inclusive spaces/
        services 121–2
    finding others that 'get' you 110
    and social anxiety 107–8
    using public spaces/services
        120–1
    validity 97–102
    see also coming out; Freiya;
        personal experiences
trauma release exercise (TRE) 182
trolls 113
truthfulness 109–10
TV 187–8

validity 32–3, 97–102
Van Den Berg, A.E. 178
Van Gogh, Vincent 15
visibility 69, 98–9
voice anxiety 77–9

waiting 141
    for gender identity services
        134
    for situations to pass 139–40
    for surgery 48, 96, 135–6

Walker, P. 144
walking 160–1, 172–4
water 184–5
weighted blankets 188
White Hughto, J.M. 36
whole grains 184
window boxes 177–8
Winfrey, Oprah 13
work
    being kind to yourself 123
    coming out at 75–6
    difficulties obtaining 44–5

personal experience 121–2
planning 123
researching 122–3
staying positive 122
writing 116, 149–50

yoga 103, 181
YouGov 121
Young, E. 54–6

Zeno of Citium 13